GW00702078

RADICAL DISCIPLESHIP

RADICAL DISCIPLESHIP

Roger Steer

14 13 12 11 10 09 08   7 6 5 4 3 2 1

Published by 10publishing, a division of 10ofthose.com
13 Airport Road, Belfast, BT3 9DY

www.10ofthose.com
Published in conjunction with OMF www.omf.org

First published by Monarch Books (a publishing imprint of Lion Hudson
PLC) in 1995 under the title of *Hudson Taylor: Lessons in Discipleship.*

British Library Cataloguing in Publication Data
A catalogue record for this book is available from the British Library

ISBN-13: 978-1-906173-01-2

Design by Jon Caplin, www.electrolyte.co.uk
Printed in Great Britain by J.H. Haynes & Co., Sparkford

Contents

Series Introduction

Jesus was supremely concerned that his followers might be both disciples and disciple makers. But in reality what does this mean? What does a true disciple look like? What does a true disciple do? What is the role of a disciple maker?

This series is designed to help Christians with those questions. Living as a disciple of Jesus Christ is not easy; there are many challenges and struggles, however, we do believe that God has equipped us with everything we need to live a life which is pleasing and honouring to Him.

In 2 Timothy Paul was able to write: '. . . the time has come for my departure. I have fought the good fight, I have finished the race, I have kept the faith. Now there is in store for me the crown of righteousness . . .'

We desire that this series might help us to be able to say the same thing when our departure from this life looms. These books seek to address some of the main issues that face a Christian disciple. The principles taught in this series are not based on good notions, but rather straightforward, biblical theology.

May it cause each of us to fight the good fight; finish the race; and keep the faith.

When it's all been said and done
There is just one thing that matters
Did I do my best to live for truth
Did I live my life for You
When it's all been said and done
All my treasures will mean nothing
Only what I've done for love's Reward
Will stand the test of time

Lord Your mercy is so great
That You look beyond our Weakness
And find purest gold in miry clay
Making sinners into saints

I will always sing Your praise
Here on earth and ever after
For You've shown me Heaven's my
True home
When it's all been said and done
You're my life when life is gone

Lord I'll live my life for You

When It's All Been Said and Done by James A. Cowan
© Copyright 1999 Integrity's Hosanna! Music/Sovereign Music UK
Reproduced by permission, sovereignmusaic@aol.com

Jonathan Carswell

Acknowledgements

I want to thank Edyth Banks (formerly of OMF's Communications Department in Singapore, now working at the Agape Family and Counselling Centre) for her patient work on an earlier version of this book, sorting out some of its more ponderous and polemical passages. The late Jim Broomhall knew of my plans to work on this project and offered me his advice and encouragement as he did with *Hudson Taylor: A Man in Christ*. I miss him. Julia Cameron and Tony Collins gave me help and valuable criticism; I pray that God will bless the publishing partnership between OMF and Monarch of which this book is one of the earliest fruits. Lastly, as ever, Sheila, Tim and Joe have kept me more or less sane and given me the strength to write this second book about the remarkable man who thought of himself as the little servant of a great Master.

Roger Steer
Down St Mary, Devon

Foreword

Lessons I Learned from Hudson Taylor

I can still remember the impact which was made on me, as an undergraduate at Cambridge University in the forties, when I read *Hudson Taylor: The Growth of a Soul* and *The Man Who Believed God*. Hudson Taylor's example challenged me, then as a student, and later as a pastor, to a greater and a wiser faith. He has always seemed to me to exemplify a robust, reasonable and realistic faith. He taught me four important aspects of Christian faith.

First, faith rests on God's faithfulness, I remember reading that Hudson Taylor liked to render Jesus' command 'have faith in God' (Mark 11:22) with the words 'reckon on the faithfulness of God'. This paraphrase, although not exegetically exact, is theologically correct. Human faith and divine faithfulness are the obverse and reverse of the same coin. It is precisely because God is faithful that faith is reasonable, for there is no more trustworthy person than God. So to trust the trustworthy is hardly daring or adventurous; it is plain, sober common sense.

Secondly, faith is the trust of a child. God is not only the Faithful One, but our Father too through Jesus

Christ. He invites us to call him 'Father' and to share our concerns and needs with him as children do with their parents. I cannot do better here than quote Hudson Taylor himself: 'I am taking my children with me, and I notice that it is not difficult for me to remember that the little ones need breakfast in the morning, dinner at mid-day, and something before they go to bed at night. Indeed, I could not forget it. And I find it *impossible* to suppose that our Heavenly Father is less tender or mindful than I.' Again, 'I do not believe that our Heavenly Father will ever forget his children. I am a very poor father, but it is not my habit to forget my children. God is a very, very good Father. It is not his habit to forget his children.'

Thirdly, faith is as necessary in the material realm as in the spiritual, that is, when needing money as much as when seeking converts. One of Hudson Taylor's best-known aphorisms was: 'God's work, done in God's way will never lack supplies.' I know there is a measure of debate about what constitutes a 'faith mission', and whether financial needs should be made known to God alone or may be disclosed to God's people also. Certainly the Apostle Paul saw nothing incongruous in urging the Greek churches to contribute to the collection which he was organising for the poverty-stricken Judean churches. But underlying his appeal was his confidence in God.

During my time at All Souls Church it has had to face two daunting and unavoidable building projects. Michael Baughen led us in the first and Richard Bewes in the second. And though the two leaders have differed from one another in style, they have been united in faith. It is from Hudson Taylor as much as from anybody else that I myself have learned the secondary importance of money. I believe strongly that if we are doing God's work according to God's will, in God's way, the necessary money will be forthcoming.

Fourthly, faith is not incompatible with the use of means. On his first voyage to China in 1853, the vessel in which Hudson Taylor was sailing was caught in a severe storm, off the coast of Wales. He had promised his mother that he would wear a life-belt. But when the captain ordered passengers to wear them, he felt it would be a sign of unbelief and thereby dishonouring to God. So he gave his away. But as he reflected on his action, he came to see his mistake. 'The use of means' he wrote, 'ought not to lessen our faith in God, and our faith in God ought not to hinder our using whatever means he has given us for the accomplishment of his own purposes.' Similarly, we might add, a farmer's trust in God is not incompatible with ploughing, sowing and reaping, nor a patient's with going to the doctor and taking medicine, nor a church leader's with necessary organisation.

To sum up, authentic faith is not a synonym for superstition or credulity or lazy inactivity. It rests on the faithfulness and the fatherliness of God, and is accompanied by sensible precautions and actions.

So I welcome the publication of *Radical Discipleship* and pray that it will stimulate many readers to emulate Hudson Taylor's faith.

Revd Dr John Stott

An Introduction into the Life of Hudson Taylor

Becoming a Christian at 17, James Hudson Taylor felt a growing conviction that God wanted him in China. Though many thought his faith foolish and his ideas unconsidered, within four years he was on the six-month voyage to Shanghai, as a member of the Chinese Evangelisation Society.

Leaving his family behind, he had no certainty he would ever return. His arrival at Shanghai was lonely, and fraught with danger and difficulty. A vicious civil war was raging. Rebels held the city and fires, famine and fearsome circumstances brought the young mission-ary to his knees. Taylor was forced to sleep on the streets and was attacked and ridiculed. But within 12 months of arriving he had seen his first convert.

Living amongst the Chinese, Taylor began to feel increasingly strongly that the only way to avoid the sus-picion and dislike that Westerners incurred was to become part of the Chinese community. He wore Chinese dress, grew a pigtail and lived the same way that the Chinese did. Other Westerners living in China mocked and insulted him, but slowly Taylor began to win the trust and respect of the Chinese he was there to reach.

Unwilling to compromise on this principle, or on the issue of looking to God only to supply his financial needs, Taylor felt he had no choice but to leave the society he had originally gone to China with, and to work as a lone agent.

Setting out on his own, he moved to Ningbo, where he met Maria Dyer. Many opposed their union, but the couple went ahead and married in 1858. The church they pastored grew to 21 members but, soon after, ill health meant they were forced to return to England.

During their time in the UK, Taylor translated the New Testament into the Ningbo dialect, completed his medical training, becoming a member of the Royal College of Surgeons and began an appeal for 24 new workers. His inspirational book *China's Spiritual Needs and Claims* had a dramatic impact across the Christian community. In 1865 Taylor founded the China Inland Mission (now OMF International) with 'ten pounds and all the promises of God.' A year later, the Taylor family sailed back to China on board the *Lammermuir*, with the first members of the newly formed CIM in tow.

Life was far from easy. In 1867 Taylor's daughter Grace died. The Yangzhou Riots saw more than 8000 Chinese mob the CIM house in anti-western feeling and in 1870, Maria, his beloved wife, died.

Hudson Taylor returned to the UK where, despite grief and physical tiredness, he set up the headquarters of the CIM. Over the next decade he made repeated trips to and from China, often plagued by ill-health and separated from his second wife, Jennie for long periods of time. New ministries were set up across China's interior, including a pioneering women's ministry. By 1881 there were 96 missionaries in the CIM. In 1885 another

70 joined them, including the illustrious Cambridge Seven.

With a vision for 100 more new workers, Hudson Taylor returned to the UK, speaking passionately across the country about the need in China. Travels to Canada, the US and Europe led to new offices being established and international members joining the mission. The call for 100 new workers was exactly met and a further call for 1000 new workers in 1890 led to 1153 missionaries joining the CIM within 5 years, despite the Sino-Japanese war. By 1890, Taylor had moved the CIM headquarters to China.

These successes were costly though, and in 1900 over-work lead to Taylor's breakdown at a conference in Boston, where, in the middle of an address, he began to repeat a sentence over and over again: 'You may trust the Lord too little, but you can never trust him too much'. He spent the subsequent years convalescing in Switzerland.

Meanwhile in China, the Boxer Rebellion martyred 58 CIM missionaries and more than 21 children. But the Chinese Church was still growing and now numbered more than 100,000. Hudson Taylor died in 1905, with over 800 missionaries at work in China and having baptised more than 18,000 Chinese Christians.

Hudson Taylor grew into one of the most profound Christian thinkers of all time. We can easily see Taylor's inspiring leadership skills; his unswerving faith; his nerve; his courage; and his readiness to work hard physically as well as mentally.

An awe-inspiring man of God, he lived an astounding life of faith, but how did an ordinary Yorkshire lad achieve all this?

Charles H. Spurgeon recalls a meeting with Hudson Taylor, 'Still not fully recovered from his injury, Taylor was lame and short, and didn't look like a man who would be selected to run a large missionary organsation. There was no self-assertion about him, but a firm trust in God. He was certain of the presence and help of God to turn aside from a chosen course of action.'

Another friend recalls, 'Taylor didn't come across like the "great man"' one had expected – he had no high and imposing airs, but rather the sort of greatness of which Christ spoke when he said the meek would inherit the earth.'

The Rev John Southey had a similar experience of Taylor. Expecting Taylor to be a striking and imposing figure, he was disappointed on meeting him. But after spending time talking with Taylor, Southey commented, 'So constantly did Taylor look to God, and so deep was his communion with God, that his very face seemed to have upon it a heavenly light. We could not help noticing the utter lack of self-assertion about him, and his true, because unconscious, humility. He had not been many hours in my house before my sense of disappointment gave place to a deep reverence and love, and I realised as never before what the grace of God could do.'

Introduction

Capturing the Essence of Christianity

Amid all the voices which clamour for our attention as we enter the twenty-first century, how do we discern truth? Jesus claimed to be the 'way, the truth and the life'[1] and thanks partly to the efforts of men like Hudson Taylor, there are more Christians alive today than ever before. What aspects of Christianity have caused it to stand the test of time while other philosophies have fallen away? Which expressions of it are most enduring? What lies at the heart of Christian faith?

This book presents one answer to these important questions based on the life experience and writings of one man. Hudson Taylor has been a major part of my life since I began work on his biography in 1985. Even after the publication of *Hudson Taylor: A Man in Christ*,[2] I continued to reflect on the significance of the man and his achievements against the background of my own struggles in Christian discipleship and studies in church history – researches which have taken me deeply into the lives and writings of Christians through the centuries from right across the church spectrum. As I have reflected on Hudson Taylor's life, I have grown convinced that the insights of this man of prayer, profound thought and action come close to capturing the essence of Christianity.

I began my reflections by asking myself what sustained Hudson Taylor along the path of his Christian pilgrimage: what made him tick? I have thought about his habit of waking before dawn to pray and read his Bible; I have recalled that he mixed with Christians of many traditions and with educated, cultured men from the other side of the world whose philosophy took no account of Jesus. I remembered how he confronted face-to-face the leaders and followers of other religions; how he coped with the daunting practical problems of building up what was to become the biggest missionary society in China; how he struggled to lead a motley crew of young and sometimes headstrong pioneers; how he overcame snobbish and prejudiced opposition from sections of the missionary establishment to his courting the girl he loved and to his donning Chinese dress; how he faced heartbreak in his own family; and how he staked his own reputation, and that of his mission and his God, on a public declaration that God would provide for their needs in the absence of appeals for funds.

In 1888 Hudson Taylor visited Canada. Wherever he preached, young people – some students – offered themselves as missionaries to China. Taylor had been opposed to the idea of establishing a branch of the China Inland Mission (CIM) in North America, but now grew convinced that it was God's will that such a branch should be established. It was reported that the 'solemn look' on his face disappeared as over forty men and women applied to join the CIM, and as crowded meetings were held in honour of eight young women and six men who were judged suitable to travel out to China. Invited to speak at one of these meetings in Toronto, a father told what it meant to part with his daughter. 'I have nothing too precious for my Lord Jesus. He has asked for my very best; I give, with all my heart, my very best for him.'

In later years, Hudson Taylor often recalled the phrase 'nothing too precious for my Lord Jesus' as one of his most treasured memories of that first visit to North America. But, as so often happens, sections of the press took a rather different view of Taylor's visit to Toronto. In fact, travelling on a train bound for Montreal, Henry Frost (whom we shall meet again) was forced to hold his breath while Hudson Taylor read a critical article he had tried to prevent him seeing. The article, about Taylor's visit to Toronto, maintained that he was 'rather disappointing'; didn't look like a great missionary; that a stranger would never notice him in the street except to think that here was a 'good-natured looking Englishman'; and that his eloquence as a public speaker fell short of Canada's best preachers. Putting the article down when he had read it, Hudson Taylor smiled at his friend. 'This is very just criticism for it is all true. I have often thought that God made me little in order that he might show what a great God he is.'

Actually, the Canadian reporter's assessment of Hudson Taylor's performance as a public speaker doesn't coincide with scores of reports from many countries which speak of his success in holding audiences spellbound throughout lengthy addresses – so we must make some allowance for the characteristic journalistic habit of 'taking a line'. Apart from this, Hudson Taylor was probably not being unduly modest to conclude that the article was 'all true'; for he was mightily used by God without possessing unusual natural gifts. What was remarkable about him was that, in Jim Packer's words, 'vision, passion, devotion, love, initiative, wisdom and sheer guts' combined, by the grace of God, to produce a hero – but a hero with whose struggles, mistakes, defeats and triumphs many have since been able to identify. They have felt that Hudson Taylor's God could make something of their faltering attempts to follow Jesus.

As the train rattled on from Toronto to Montreal, Henry Frost and Hudson Taylor climbed into their sleeping berths, Frost above Taylor. Frost thought about the remarkable man who lay beneath him. *'It is not hard for a little man to try to be great; but it is very hard for a great man to try to be little. Mr Taylor, however . . . has entered into that humility which alone is found in the spirit of the lowly Nazarene.'* In his epilogue to my earlier book, Hudson Taylor's great-grandson, James Hudson Taylor III, then General Director of OMF (formally CIM), wrote: 'The lessons in discipleship highlighted in *Hudson Taylor: A Man in Christ* are not limited to a man or the organisation he founded. They are abiding principles that can be learned and lived by any Christian, whether student or home-maker, employer or employee. The key is to act on them.' Those words persuaded me that this book was needed.

Some of the lessons in discipleship referred to by Dr Taylor are woven into the narrative of *A Man in Christ.* This new book, as well as making the lessons more accessible and easy to identify, also draws on source material which was inappropriate for the biography and therefore includes many of Taylor's insights which didn't find a place in my earlier work.

I have identified what I believe are the key lessons which we can learn from Hudson Taylor's life and writings. They are, in Dr Taylor's words, 'abiding principles' highly relevant for Christians today, though often controversial, always demanding, and often unfashionable. But I believe that the following pages, in taking us to the heart of Hudson Taylor's faith, also lead us to the place where God's love shines brightest of all – the cross of Calvary.

Former Archbishop, George Carey, has said that 'the Spirit-filled servant cannot be denied a ministry different from that which his Spirit-filled Master passed through . . . Often following Christ will take us into suffering and hardship, and his Spirit is as much there as he is in the smooth and pleasant places.' Hudson Taylor's remarkable life took him through suffering and hardship as well as along pleasant paths, through deep sorrow as well as ecstatic joy. Certainly there was for him no easy route to victorious Christian living; you'll find no hint of a bland triumphalism in this book.

Calvary, where Jesus died, warmed Hudson Taylor's heart with the thought of God's infinite love, grace and forgiveness; but the cross also gave him a clue as to the sort of pathway he had been called to walk along. And the cross spoke to him of how seriously God took sin: there would surely have been no need for Jesus to die if sin were of little consequence.

So like John Wesley, who was once entertained by Taylor's great grandfather, Hudson Taylor took sin seriously. If a candidate for the mission field didn't mean to 'walk blamelessly'[3] Hudson Taylor thought that he or she had better stay at home. Christians, he said, shouldn't break one of the least of God's commandments; they shouldn't tolerate the thought of impurity. Sin, even if forgiven, isn't undone – its consequences remain.

Hudson Taylor held an optimistic view of the heights of holiness to which men and women created in the image of God, redeemed and renewed, can rise.

He knew that walking where Jesus walked would take the disciple along the path of suffering. The cross, he said, doesn't usually get more comfortable along the way – but it bears sweet fruit. To carry the cross is to die daily. Sometimes fuller blessing comes through deeper suffering. God who sends the trial gives the needed grace. Come joy or come sorrow, we take it from God; and the glorious truth of the resurrection reminds us that light out of darkness is God's order.

Hudson Taylor knew that China would never be won by quiet, ease-loving men and women. Everything in Christ's service has a cost. But the rewards, in this life as much as in the next, are great. Cross-bearing doesn't mean anxiety. God wants us to enjoy his perfect peace: we should be unburdened, fully supplied, strong and happy. There's no work which is so royally rewarded as the service of God.

In his book *The Cost of Discipleship*,[4] Dietrich Bonhoeffer wrote: 'Cheap grace is the deadly enemy of our church. We are fighting today for costly grace. Cheap grace is the preaching of forgiveness without requiring repentance, baptism without church discipline, communion without confession, absolution without personal confession. Cheap grace is grace without discipleship, grace without the cross.' I don't know whether Bonhoeffer ever read any of Hudson Taylor's writings, but if he did, there can be no doubt that he would have acquitted him of the charge of 'cheap grace'. The lessons of Hudson Taylor's life provide a vivid reminder that genuine discipleship is radical discipleship – the costly way of the cross.

If you think that Hudson Taylor's lessons in discipleship are too demanding, or if you don't agree with them, I'd love to hear from you. You can contact me either through OMF International whose address is given on page 98 or through 10publishing. The glimpses of Hudson Taylor which have been highlighted in this introduction, and throughout the book, reveal the sort of man this set of beliefs produced, and how he came across to others.

1.

An Unshakeable Conviction

The Life of Faith Begins

In June 1849, when Hudson Taylor was seventeen, his mother locked herself in a room fifty miles from home. Unknown to her son, she resolved that afternoon not only to pray that Hudson would become a Christian, but to stay in the room until she was sure her prayers had been answered.

That very afternoon Hudson picked up a tract, read it, fell on his knees and accepted Jesus and his salvation. He realised for the first time the full significance of the Saviour's cry from the cross 'It is finished'. As he wrote soon afterwards, he came to see that Calvary meant a 'full and perfect atonement and satisfaction for sin: the debt was paid by the substitute. Christ died for my sins.'

It was a wonderful day, an answer to both his mother's and his sister's prayers. But it was only a beginning. For the next fifty-six years, the life of faith involved many struggles, triumphs, heartaches and perplexities.

Strengthening Spiritual Muscles

Three years after his conversion, Hudson Taylor told his mother that he felt called to travel to China as a missionary as soon as possible. In preparation, he lived as cheaply as he could, giving away about sixty per cent of his small earnings. In addition, he decided that his 'spiritual muscles' needed strengthening. *When I get to China*, he thought, *I shall have no claim on anyone for anything: my only claim will be on God. How important, therefore, to learn before leaving England to move men, through God, by prayer alone.*

And so he embarked on a series of experiments with God.

When his employer, surgeon Robert Hardey, asked him to remind him whenever his salary was due, Hudson Taylor took this as a cue never to speak to him about pay, but to ask God to do the reminding. This led to narrow and exciting scrapes, but in the end he always received his salary in the nick of time. And after giving away his last half-crown to a starving Irish labourer, he felt that God rewarded his step of faith when a gold half-sovereign arrived for him in the following day's post.

Learning of the Love of God

Hudson Taylor left England for the first time and sailed for China in 1853, when he was not yet twenty-one. 'My mother went with me into the little cabin that was to be my home for nearly six months. We parted, and she went on shore, giving me her blessing. I stood on the deck and she followed the ship as we moved towards the dock gates. As we passed the gates, and the separation was commencing, I shall never forget the cry of anguish that was wrung from my mother's heart as she felt that I was gone. It went to my heart like a knife. I never knew so fully as then what "God so loved the world" meant: and I am quite sure that my precious mother learned more of the love of God for the world in that hour than in all her life before.

'Oh friends! When we are brought into the position of having practical fellowship with God in trial and sorrow and suffering, we learn a lesson that is not to be learnt amidst the ease and comfort of ordinary life. That is why God so often brings us through trying experiences.'

The Demand for Obedience

Hudson Taylor didn't believe it made any sense to draw a distinction between having Christ as Saviour and having him as Lord. For him, lordship, with its demand for obedience, was fundamental to what being a Christian was all about.

Reflecting on the meaning of Christ's words in Mark 16:15, 'Go into all the world and preach the good news to all creation', he wrote:

'How are we to treat the Lord Jesus Christ in reference to this command? Shall we definitely drop the title Lord as applied to him, and take the ground that we are quite willing to recognise him as Saviour, so far as the eternal penalty of sin is concerned, but are not prepared to recognise ourselves as bought with a price, or him as having any claim to our unquestioning obedience? Shall we say that we are our own masters, willing to recognise something as his due, provided he does not ask too much?

'The heart of every true Christian will unhesitatingly reject this proposition when so formulated, but have not countless lives in each generation been lived as though it were a proper ground to take? How few of the Lord's people have recognised the truth that Christ is either Lord of all, or is not Lord at all. "Why do you call me, 'Lord, Lord,' and do not do what I say?" (Luke 6:46). Shall it not become our holy ambition to all who have health and youth to court the Master's approval and tread in his steps, in seeking to save a lost world? And shall not Christian parents encourage their enthusiasm?'

At Home with One Sheep?

'When will it dawn on the Lord's people', Hudson Taylor wondered, 'that God's command to preach the gospel to every creature was not intended for the wastepaper basket?' Early in 1865, when back in England after his first term in China, he wrote a small book which came to have an enormous influence, *China: Its Spiritual Need and Claims*. He prayed about every paragraph he wrote. The result didn't make comfortable reading if you were a Christian who favoured a cosy life:

'Can the Christians of England sit still with folded arms while these multitudes are perishing – perishing for lack of knowledge – for lack of that knowledge which England possesses so richly, which has made England what England is, and made us what we are? What does the Master teach us? Is it not that if one sheep out of a hundred be lost, we are to leave the ninety and nine and seek that one? But here the proportions are exactly reversed, and we stay at home with the one sheep, and take no heed of the ninety and nine perishing ones!

'Christian brethren, think of the imperative command of our great Captain and Leader, "Go into all the world and preach the good news to all creation": think of all the millions of poor benighted in China to whom no loving follower of the self-renouncing One has brought good news …'

The book may have hurt to read, but it proved a bestseller. It was reprinted many times and by 1887 had already gone into seven editions.

2

'Why Didn't You Come Sooner?'

An Embarrassing Question

Among those who heard Hudson Taylor preach at the Bridge Street Chapel in Ningbo, China in 1858 was Ni Yongfa, a cotton dealer and leader of a reformed Buddhist sect which would have nothing to do with idolatry and was searching for truth. At the end of Hudson's sermon, Ni stood at his place and turned to address the audience.

'I have long searched for the truth as my father did before me. I have travelled far, but I haven't found it. I found no rest in Confucianism, Buddhism or Daoism, but I do find rest in what I have heard tonight. From now on I believe in Jesus.'

Ni took Hudson Taylor to a meeting of the sect he had formerly led and was allowed to explain the reasons for his change of faith. Taylor was impressed with the clarity and power with which he spoke. Another member of the group was converted and both he and Ni were baptised.

'How long has the gospel been known in England?' Ni asked Hudson Taylor.

'For several hundred years,' replied an embarrassed Hudson Taylor vaguely.

'What!' exclaimed Ni. 'And you have only now come to preach it to us? My father sought after the truth for more than twenty years and died without finding it. Why didn't you come sooner?'

It was a difficult question to answer.

A Man Apart

From March 1854 until his resignation in May 1857, Hudson Taylor worked in China as an agent of the Chinese Evangelisation Society. Hudson continued his work from 1857 in China as an independent missionary.

On his return to England, he successfully qualified as a member of the Royal College of Surgeons, passed the Licentiate in Midwifery and edited the Ningbo colloquial *New Testament*.

In the spring of 1865, he nearly went out of his mind weighing up the possibility of establishing a new agency for the evangelisation of inland China. For months so many thoughts and concerns raced around in his mind that he rarely slept for more than two hours at a time, sometimes not at all.

He was invited to Brighton for the weekend of 24-26 June, 'and on the Sunday morning went to church and was moved by the sermon.' Then, as he recalled:

'Unable to bear the sight of a congregation of a thousand or more Christian people rejoicing in their own security, while millions were perishing for lack of knowledge, I wandered out on the sands alone, in great spiritual agony; and there the Lord conquered my unbelief, and I surrendered

> myself to God for this service. I told him that all the responsibility as to the issues and consequences must rest with him; that as his servant it was mine to obey and to follow him – his to direct, to care for, and to guide me and those who might labour with me.'

He prayed for 'twenty-four willing, skilful labourers' who would join him in forming the basis of the new China Inland Mission (CIM).

This vivid picture of Hudson Taylor's agony contrasted with the apathy of the cosy congregation, sums up well the sense in which he was a man apart – totally committed to the service of Christ.

A Team to Share His Commitment

The twenty-four 'willing, skilful labourers' Hudson prayed for were intended to be two for each of the eleven provinces which until then were without a missionary, and two for Mongolia. The qualities he was looking for in the men and women who would make up the first two dozen CIM missionaries differed somewhat from those sought by other societies. The Church Missionary Society and the London Missionary Society wanted ordained men, preferably from the universities. So Hudson Taylor took care not to draw away such men from their church societies.

He wanted intelligent, educated men and women, but was convinced that the crucial factor was the candidate's spiritual qualities. The door would be open to those with little formal education. And the most important spiritual quality needed would be the unshakeable conviction that there was a faithful God – coupled with the ability and willingness to trust him.

Few of the other societies gave much scope to women except as school teachers. From the outset, the CIM was to be open to women of the right kind – and the younger they were the quicker they would learn the language. Women would have an indispensable role in working with Chinese women.

The new recruits would have to accept Hudson and his wife Maria Taylor as their leaders: they were the only ones with experience in living and working in China. In exchange, Hudson Taylor would give them basic preliminary training and provide them with suitable clothing.

Men and Women who Trust God's Promises

The sort of men and women Hudson Taylor looked for to join the ranks of the CIM were, in his words:

'Fellow-believers, irrespective of denomination, who fully believe in the inspiration of God's Word, and are willing to prove their faith by going into inland China with only the guarantees they carry within the covers of their pocket Bibles. Jesus said, "Seek first his kingdom and his righteousness, and all these things [food and clothes] will be given you as well."[5] If anyone does not believe that God speaks the truth, it would be better for him not to go to China to propagate the faith. If he does believe it, surely the promise will be all he needs.

'If anyone does not mean to walk blamelessly,[6] he had better stay at home; if he does mean to walk blamelessly, he has all he needs in the shape of a guarantee fund. God owns all the gold and silver in the world, and the cattle on a thousand hills. We need not be vegetarians.

'Money wrongly placed, and money given from wrong motives, are both to be greatly dreaded. We can afford to have as little as the Lord chooses to give; but we cannot afford to have unconsecrated money, or to have money placed in the wrong position. Far better to have no money at all, even to buy food with, for there are ravens in China which the Lord can send again with bread and flesh. The Lord is always faithful; he tries the faith of his people, or rather their faithfulness.

'People say, "Lord, increase our faith". Did not the Lord rebuke his disciples for that prayer?[7] He said, "You do not want a great faith, but faith in a great God. If your faith were as small as a grain of mustard seed, it would suffice to remove this mountain!" We need faith that rests in a great God, and which expects him to keep his Word, and to do just what he has promised.'

A Unique Mission

Taylor intended that the CIM would have six distinctive features. First, its missionaries would be drawn not from any particular denomination but from all the leading Christian churches – provided they could sign a simple doctrinal declaration. In practice, as the mission developed, they would come from many different countries too.

Second, the missionaries would have no guaranteed salary, but trust in the Lord to supply their needs. Income would be shared. No debts would be incurred.

Third, no appeals for funds would be made; there would be no collectors; the names of donors wouldn't be published; instead each would receive a dated and numbered receipt by which he would be able to trace his own contribution in the list of donations and then into the annually published accounts.

Fourth, anxious to learn from the mistakes made by the Chinese Evangelisation Society with whom he had first gone to China, Hudson Taylor was determined that the work abroad would be directed not by home committees, but by himself and eventually other leaders on the spot in China.

Fifth, the activities of the mission would be systematic and practical. A comprehensive plan to evangelise the whole of China would seek to establish footholds in strategic centres. The aim would not be to secure the largest number of converts for the CIM, but rather to bring about as quickly as possible the evangelisation of the whole of China. Who actually garnered the sheaves would be regarded as of secondary importance.

Sixth, as a courtesy to the Chinese people, the missionaries would wear Chinese clothes and worship in buildings in the Chinese style.

'The Wind Will Never Waft It!'

In June 1872, Taylor shared the platform at the annual Mildmay Conference with D.L. Moody. Lustily the congregation sang 'Waft, waft ye winds his story' and then settled back into their seats eager to hear the founder of the China Inland Mission speak. Hudson Taylor stood up with a twinkle in his eye but a serious point to make.

'My dear friends,' he said, 'the wind will never waft it! If the blessed story of his love is to be taken to the dark places of the earth, it must be taken by men and women like ourselves . . . who wish to obey the great missionary command.'

3.

Knowing God

His Concept of God

Hudson Taylor trusted God. He believed, as have so many great men and women of faith that Christians should be taken up less with the nature of faith and more with the reality of God. 'You do not need a great faith, but faith in a great God.' What, then, was his concept of God? Hudson Taylor's insights into the nature of God, his character and ways, were illuminated by his interest in the laws of science. His starting point was to urge people never to forget three important statements: 'There is a God; he has spoken to us in the Bible; he means what he says.'

The God of Nature

He stressed that God was the God of nature as well as of grace and it followed from this that none of God's ways were arbitrary:

'All the acts and all the requirements of perfect wisdom and of perfect goodness must of necessity be wise and good. As God always acts in the *best* way, so, in the same circumstances, he always acts in the same way. The uniformity of his mode of action in nature is seen and recognised by many who do not know the great Actor. Such often prefer to speak of the constancy of the laws of nature, rather than of the uniformity of the operations of God. But if we speak of the laws of nature, let us not misunderstand the expression. It is the law of a well-regulated household that the door is opened when the door bell is rung. It would be an entire mistake, however, to suppose that this is done by the law: it is done, no matter whether directly or mediately, by the head of the household . . . So one sparrow will not "fall to the ground apart from the will of your Father." [8]

'We who know God, and are his children, do well to remind ourselves that it is *our unchanging* God who makes water on the fire to boil, and the steam in the engine to develop such expansive power: that it is he who acts uniformly in electricity, whether we avail ourselves of his power in the useful telegraph, or succumb to it in the fatal thunderbolt: and that it is *his uniform action* that we recognise as the law of gravitation.'

The God of Grace

'No less constant and sovereign is he in the domain of grace: his sovereignty is never erratic or arbitrary. His method of action may be studied and largely discovered in spiritual things as in natural. Some of his laws are plainly revealed in his Word; others are exemplified in the actions recorded therein. And best of all, by the illumination of the Holy Spirit, God himself may be known, and loved, and revered through the study of his written Word: and he is especially seen in the face of Jesus Christ ...

'As in natural things there are many mysteries beyond the understanding of feeble man: so also in spiritual things there are things not yet revealed, not intended to be known here and now. But just as by utilising what may be known, and is known in nature, men achieve great results – as by steam, electricity and so on – so by utilising what is revealed and may be known in spiritual things, great results can be achieved. Ten thousand horses could not convey the loads from London to Glasgow in a week that are easily taken half a day by rail; ten thousand couriers could not convey the news from London to Shanghai in months that may now be flashed by cable, in a few hours. And so in spiritual things no amount of labour and machinery will accomplish without spiritual power, what may easily be accomplished when we place ourselves in the current of God's will, and work by his direction, in his way.'

Practical Knowledge

Hudson Taylor always made the link between an intellectual understanding of Christian truth and its practical application to our daily lives. And so he wrote that, 'there is a far closer connection than we sometimes realise between the knowledge of God and practical use of that knowledge.'

Commenting on the words of John 17:3, 'Now this is eternal life: that they may know you, the only true God, and Jesus Christ whom you have sent', he said:

'It is just as we are faithfully living out the life he has put in us, and faithfully using the knowledge given to us, that we learn practically to know him. We cannot separate these things if we want to know the power of his resurrection, we must also know the fellowship of his sufferings, being made conformable to his death. There must be the living out of the life of God in order that we may learn to know him more fully and perfectly. We only know and understand that through which we have passed.'

The Gospel of the Kingdom

Hudson Taylor regretted that in his day the phrase 'the gospel of the kingdom' was seldom used, and that, when it was, it was little more than a meaningless phrase. And yet, he said, the Bible was full of the blessings brought by and enjoyed under God's rule. Maybe he was reacting against the dispensational teaching which interpreted Christ's teaching on the kingdom as applying only to a future age.

'Let us then prize this great truth of the Kingship of the Lord Jesus, meditate upon it, and act upon it. The New Testament as well as the Old bears abundant witness to it. The angel announced before his birth, "The Lord God will give him the throne of his father David, and he will reign over the house of Jacob for ever; his kingdom will never end.[9] To Pilate, the Lord himself bore witness:

'My kingdom is not of this world ...'
'You are a king, then!'
'For this reason I was born.'"[10]

'Born to reign, he acted consistently throughout his life of ministry. As a king he called his apostles authoritatively to leave their properties and employments and follow him. As a king he laid down the laws of the kingdom in the Sermon on the Mount. And as a king he despatched his ambassadors to preach the gospel of the kingdom. With royal dignity he witnessed before his sacrificial death to his kingship; the title over the cross proclaimed it, and he was raised as Prince and Saviour.'

Hold God's Faithfulness

These days many people regard faith as simple-mindedness and as the expression of an uncritical spirit which is inappropriate to twenty-first century men and women. The Bible, on the other hand, portrays faith as stepping forward not into darkness but into God's light and truth.

In Mark 11:22 it is recorded that Jesus said to his disciples, 'Have faith in God'. He went on to tell them that if anyone says to a mountain, 'Go, throw yourself into the sea' and doesn't doubt in his heart but believes that what he says will happen, it will be done. On the basis of a careful study of the original Greek text and a comparison with other related passages, Hudson Taylor liked to render the three words in Mark 11:22, 'Hold God's faithfulness'. Encouraging readers to remain faithful, Hudson Taylor urged: 'Let us see that in theory we *hold* that God is faithful; that in daily life we *count* upon it; and that at all times and under all circumstances we are fully *persuaded* of this blessed truth.'

An Inspired Creed

Hudson Taylor believed that the three words 'hold God's faithfulness' amounted to an inspired creed:

> 'Short, intelligible, and to the point. It meets every man's need, is suitable to every age and to every country, and appropriate in every circumstance of daily life. It bears on all man's temporal affairs; it meets his every spiritual want.
>
> 'To God's faithfulness we should look for our necessary food – "give us this day our daily bread". To him, too, should we look for clothes, for he clothes the lilies of the field. Every care for temporal things we should bring to him, and then be careful for nothing. To him likewise should we come with all spiritual want, that we may obtain mercy, and find grace to help in time of need. Is our path dark? He is our sun. Are we in danger? He is our shield. If we trust in him, we shall not be put to shame; but if our faith fails, he will not. "If we are faithless, he will remain faithful."[11]
>
> 'Want of trust is at the root of almost all our sins and all our weakness; and how shall we escape from it, but by looking at him, and observing his faithfulness? As the light which shines from the dark waters of the lake is the reflection of the sun's rays, so man's faith is the impress and reflection of God's faith. The man who holds God's faith will not be reckless or foolhardy, but he will be ready for every emergency. The man who holds God's faith will dare obey him, however impolitic it may appear.'

But just as men and women need a creed, so Hudson Taylor warned that Satan has his creed: 'Doubt God's faithfulness. Has God said? Are you not mistaken as to his commands? He could not really mean so. You take an extreme view – give too literal meaning to the words.' Ah! How constantly, and alas, how successfully, are such arguments used to prevent whole-hearted trust in God, whole-hearted consecration to God. 'All God's giants have been weak men, who did great things for God because they reckoned on God being with them.'

What is Faith?

Hudson Taylor believed that many Christians, including himself, felt a great deal of unnecessary difficulty about faith:

'What is faith? Is it not simply the recognition of the reliability or the trustworthiness of those with whom we have to do? Why do we accept with confidence a government bond? Because we believe in the reliability of the government. Men do not hesitate to put faith in government securities, because they believe in the government that guarantees them.

'Why do we, without hesitation, put coins into circulation, instead of as in China, getting a lump sum of silver weighed and its purity investigated, before we can negotiate any money transaction with it? Because the government issues the coin we use and we use it with confidence and without difficulty.

'Why do we take a railway guide and arrange a particular journey, or even, as I am doing, arrange a journey which will extend for many months, and include Tasmania, New Zealand, and America? Well, one has confidence in the reliability of these official publications. As a rule we are not put to shame!

'Now just as we use a railway guide we must use our Bible. We must depend on God's Word just as we depend on man's word, only remembering that although a man may not be able to carry out his promise, God will always fulfil what he has said. We must exercise the same confidence towards God as towards one another. Without confidence in one another, the business and commerce of the world would be impossible. Confidence in God is equally indispensable.

'There are the two sides of faith. There is the Godward side, and there is the manward side. It is when God's faithfulness is fully recognised by us that we shall be enabled to rest in quiet confidence and faith that he will fulfil his Word.'

4.

God's Work Done in God's Way

Only God to Look to

Hudson Taylor firmly believed that God would provide for him and the mission he founded. This belief dated from not long after his conversion. In 1849 he heard that Barnsley's congregational minister had a copy of a book on China, and decided to try to borrow it.

'You may certainly borrow the book,' the minister told him. 'And what, may I ask, is your interest in it?'

'God has called me to spend my life in missionary service in China,' Hudson Taylor replied.

'And how do you propose to go there?'

'I don't know. But I think it likely that I shall need to go as the twelve and seventy disciples did in Judea, without stick, or bag, or food, or money – relying on him who had sent them to supply all their needs.'

The minister gently placed his hand on Hudson's shoulder. 'Ah, my boy, as you grow older you will become wiser than that. Such an idea would have done very well in the days when Christ himself was on earth, but not now.'

Many years later, Taylor recalled the incident and wrote: 'I have grown older since then, but not wiser. I am more and more convinced that if we were to take the directions of our

Master and the assurance he gave to his first disciples more fully as our guide, we should find them just as suited to our times as to those in which they were originally given.'

No Appeals

One of the reasons why Hudson Taylor adopted a policy of never appealing for funds – 'non-solicitation' – was that he was anxious to avoid diverting money from the established missionary societies to the CIM. Like George Muller, who became a close friend and supporter, he never attacked or criticised the financial principles of other missions or claimed that the CIM's policy was necessarily better or more biblical.

Hudson Taylor believed: 'If our hearts are right we may count upon the Holy Spirit's working through us to bring others into deeper fellowship with God – the way the work began at Pentecost. We do not need to say much about the CIM. Let people see God working, let God be glorified, let believers be made holier, happier, brought nearer to him, and they will not need to be asked to help.'

In his book *From Faith to Faith*,[12] Daniel Bacon has concluded that the 'policy of non-solicitation was to encourage in part the giving of dedicated gifts from dedicated donors. Taylor also saw it as a way to liberate the missionary from anxiety regarding the financial outcome of meetings and services. As Taylor described it: 'The missionary is then free in spirit, occupied with God rather than men, and more eager to give than to get.'

No Collections

On several occasions Taylor intervened in public meetings to forbid well-meaning chairmen from taking up collections. For example, in May 1866, he was speaking at a meeting in Totteridge, north London. The announcement of the meeting had said 'No Collection'. But when Taylor finished speaking, the chairman, Colonel Puget, tried to overrule this:

'I feel that many of you would be distressed if you were not given an opportunity to contribute to the work in China, so I trust Mr Taylor will not object to a collection being taken.'

Mr Taylor however quickly jumped to his feet:

'Mr Chairman, I beg you to keep to the conditions you agreed to. Among the reasons for making no collection, the reason put forward by your kind self is, to my mind, one of the strongest. My wish is not that members of the audience should be relieved of making such contribution as might now be convenient, under the influence of emotion, but that they should go home burdened with the deep need of China, and ask God what he would have them to do. If after thought and prayer they are satisfied that a gift of money is what he wants of them, it can be given to any missionary society having agents in China; or it may be posted to our London office. But in many cases what God wants is not a money contribution, but personal consecration to his service abroad; or the giving up of a son or a daughter – more precious than silver or gold – to his service. I think a collection tends to leave the impression that the all-important thing is money, whereas no amount of money can convert a single soul. What is needed is that men and women filled with the Holy Spirit should give themselves to the work. There'll never be a short-age of funds for the support of such people.'

Colonel Puget reluctantly agreed to abandon the collection, and Taylor stayed the night at his home. Next morning, the Colonel came down late to breakfast and admitted that he hadn't had a good night.

'Here are the contributions to your work which I was handed last night. Yesterday evening I thought you were wrong about the collection. I am now convinced you were right. As I thought through the night of the streams of souls in China ever passing into the dark, I could only cry as you suggested, "Lord, what will you have me do?" I think I have obtained the guidance I sought, and here it is.'

Colonel Puget handed Hudson Taylor a cheque for five hundred pounds. 'If there had been a collection I would have given a few pounds to it!'

Five hundred pounds would be worth well over ten thousand pounds at today's values. Over twenty years later, Hudson Taylor dared to do the same thing at the YMCA auditorium in Chicago, USA. This time, in September 1888, the chairman was the formidable international evangelist, D.L. Moody. After Hudson Taylor had intervened to prevent a collection being taken up on Moody's instructions, advancing similar reasons that he had given in London, Moody relented and exclaimed, 'Well, you are the first man I ever met who refused a good collection!'

This incident, too, had its sequel. A Christian businessman left the meeting glad that the twenty-dollar note he had intended to donate stayed in his wallet. But after a sleepless night and a troublesome conscience he sent off a five hundred dollar cheque to be used in the evangelisation of inland China.

A Hazardous Experiment

In 1887, when the CIM was twenty-two years old, Taylor looked back and described God's faithfulness in providing for the mission in answer to prayer alone. He acknowledged that many people might see it as a 'hazardous experiment to send evangelists to a distant heathen land with "only God to look to".' But as he reminded readers of *China's Spiritual Need and Claims*, he had seen God, 'in answer to prayer, quell the raging storm, alter the direction of the wind, and give rain in the midst of prolonged drought. In answer to prayer, stay the angry passions and murderous intentions of violent men, and bring the machinations of his people's foes to nought. 'In answer to prayer, raise the dying from the bed of death, when human aid was vain . . .

'For more than twenty-seven years he proved the faithfulness of God in supplying pecuniary means for his own temporal wants and for the need of the work he has been engaged in. He had seen God, in answer to prayer, raise up labourers not a few for his vast mission field; supplying the "means requisite for their outfit, passage and support; vouchsafing blessing on the efforts of many of them, both among the native Christians and the heathen Chinese in fourteen out of the eighteen provinces."'

The Great Treasurer Never Fails

One effect of the war between China and Japan in 1894 was a dramatic increase in taxation and inflation. 'This,' Hudson Taylor recorded, 'has been a source of some embarrassment':

'Where the work has been commenced on the ground that we had funds in hand, we have found that the funds have altered their value before the work was completed. Well, I need to tell you that in every case we had recourse, may I say it reverently? – To our great Treasurer, the Lord himself, and he has not failed us, and never will fail us, though the expense of living in China is increasing considerably, and the number to be supplied is increasing also. The great resources of our great God are undiminished, and we rest upon them with a full assurance that his Word is as true now as it has ever been. Our business is to "seek first the kingdom of God and his righteousness"[13] and all these things shall be added unto us.'

How Bad were the Hard Times?

Certainly the CIM went through times of financial severity. The mission's faith was fully tested, for example, in 1874-75. How serious were these times of stringency and what was the nature of the hardships endured? One donor to the mission, appropriately named Mrs Rich, wrote to say she had heard a rumour that CIM missionaries were frequently so poor that they had to give up the work and take secular employment.

Hudson Taylor replied swiftly, asking Mrs Rich to show her informant his reply. 'He has been entirely misled . . . I do not believe that any child or member of the family of anyone connected with our mission has ever lacked food or clothes for a single hour, though, in many cases the supply may not come *before* it was needed. *No-one* has been hindered in the work by lack of funds; no-one has ever suffered in health from this cause; *no-one* has ever left the mission on this ground, or has remained

dissatisfied on this score, to my knowledge . . .' He con-
ceded that there had been 'periods of stringency' but
argued that these had stirred up the Chinese to give
their own money to spread the gospel, rather than thinking that rich societies could do it. He explained why var-
ious members of the mission had left or been dismissed
– in no case for financial reasons. Mrs Rich resumed her
support.

The fact that Hudson Taylor was able to command
loyal and continuing support from his fellow missionaries – often till they died at an advanced age – suggests that
the hardships were not unduly severe and that the CIM
team were united in viewing the difficult times as trials of
faith rather than as failures on God's part to provide.

Looking to the Living God

Even when funds barely kept up with outgoings, Hudson
Taylor still envisaged expansion of the work as long as he
was convinced that he knew God's will. 'Not to advance,'
he wrote, 'would be to retreat from the position of faith
taken up at the beginning. It would be to look at difficulties rather than at the living God. True, funds were low –
had been for years, and the workers coming out from
home few, while several retirements had taken place in
China. Difficulties were formidable; and it was easy to
say, 'All these things are indications that for the present
no further expansion is possible. But not to go forward
would be to throw away opportunities God had given.'

Both Hudson Taylor and George Muller were driven
by their non-solicitation policies; first, daily to examine
their own lives as they took seriously Bible verses like
Psalm 66:18, 'If I had cherished sin in my heart, the Lord
would not have listened' and Psalm 84:11, 'No good

thing does he withhold from those whose walk is blameless'; and, second, to check that no aspect of their work hindered God's blessing and provision. Daniel Bacon rightly draws attention, too, to Taylor's strong sense of stewardship, 'believing that every gift to the mission was the outcome of a divinely given impulse.'

Working with God

Much of Hudson Taylor's writing emphasises the principle of what he called 'working with God'. The phrase captures the two vital elements of, on the one hand, God's power and, on the other, our trustful response of practical service. He often quoted Philippians 4:6; 'Do not be anxious about anything, but in everything, by prayer and petition, present your requests to God.'

'If the work is at the command of God,' he argued, 'then we go to him with full confidence for workers. And when God gives workers, then we can go to him for the means. We always accept a suitable worker, whether we have the funds or not. Then we very often say, "Now, dear friend, your first work will be to join with us in praying for money to send you to China." As soon as there is money enough, the time of the year and other circumstances being suitable, the friend goes out. We do not wait until there is a remittance in hand to give him when he gets there. The Lord will provide that.

'Our Father is a very experienced one: he knows very well that his children wake up with a good appetite every morning, and he always provides breakfast for them; and he does not send his children supperless to bed ... He sustained three million Israelites in the wilderness for forty years. We do not expect that he will send three million missionaries to China; but if he did, he would have plenty of means to sustain them. Let us see that we keep God before our eyes; that we walk in his ways, and seek to please and glorify him in everything. Depend upon it; God's work done in God's way will never lack God's supplies.' He continued: 'When the supplies do not come in, it is time to inquire: "What is wrong"? It may be only a temporary trial of faith, but if there be faith it will bear trying and if not it is well that we should not be deceived. It is very easy, with money in the pocket and food in the cupboard, to think you have faith in God. Miss Havergal says: "Those who trust him wholly find him wholly true'" But my experience proves that to those who do not trust him wholly, he does not break his Word. "He cannot disown himself".'[14]

Hudson Taylor argued that the very existence of the CIM was a visible proof of God's faithfulness in answer to prayer. 'The Mission was born of prayer, nourished by prayer, and is still sustained month by month only in answer to believing prayer.'

'. . . As to funds, we saw long ago that we had the divine warrant to go forward in the Lord's work resting on his words in Matthew 6:33. And today we rest upon his promise and are not disappointed. We do not publish donors' names, we make no collection, we have no reserve funds, and we never go into debt: our path now is as much walking on the waters as it was in the beginning. Have we not great cause to praise God?'

Simply Trusting Like a Child

When, in the spring of 1897, Hudson Taylor met leading German ministers and missionary society secretaries in the Berlin drawing room of the Baroness von Dungern, several of those present were sceptical about his mission and the notion of fundraising by faith. He disarmed their, at times, hostile questions with characteristic humility.

'I am not specially gifted' he told them, 'and am shy by nature. But my gracious and merciful God and Father inclined himself to me, and I who was weak in faith he strengthened while I was still young. He taught me in my helplessness to rest on him, and to pray about little things in which another might have felt able to help himself . . . He knew the desire of my heart, and simply trusting like a child, I brought all to him in prayer. Thus I experienced, quite early, how he is willing to help and strengthen and to fulfil the desire of those who fear him. And so in later years, when I prayed the money came.'

A Promise of True Prosperity

Hudson Taylor said that Psalm 1:3 amounted to one of the most remarkable and inclusive promises in the Bible. The man who delights in the law of the Lord is described in the verse as 'like a tree planted by streams of water, which yields its fruit in season and whose leaf does not wither. Whatever he does prospers.'

'If we could offer to the ungodly a worldly plan which would ensure their prospering in all that they undertake, how eagerly they would undertake it! And yet when God reveals so effectual a plan to his people, how few avail themselves of it! Many fail on the negative side and do not come clearly out of the world; many fail on the positive side and allow other duties and indulgences to take time that should be given to the Word of God. To some it is not at all easy to secure time for the morning watch, but nothing can make up for the loss of it. Let us now consider what the blessings are:

- **Stability:** He shall be like a tree (not a mere annual) of steady progressive growth and increasing fruitfulness.
- **Independent supplies:** "Planted by the rivers of water". The ordinary supplies of rain and dew may fail, his deep and hidden sources cannot.
- **Seasonal fruitfulness:** There is something very beautiful in this. The figure is not that of water flowing through a channel; but of fruit, the very outcome of our own transformed life – a life of union with Christ. It is so gracious of God not to work through us in a mere mechanical way, but to make us branches of the true vine, the very organ by which its fruit is produced.

    There is a fundamental difference between fruit and work. Work is the outcome of effort; fruit of life. A bad man can do good work, but a bad tree cannot bear good fruit. The result of work is not reproductive, but fruit has its need in itself. It is interesting to notice that the Scriptures do not speak of the fruits of the Spirit in the plural, as though we might take our choice among the graces named, but of the fruit in the singular, which is a rich cluster composed of love, joy, peace, long-suffering and so on. How blessed to bring forth such fruit in its season!

- **Continued vigour:** "Whose leaf does not wither". In our own climate many trees are able to maintain their life through the winter, but unable to retain their leaves.

The hardy evergreen, however, not only lives, but maintains its leaf, and all the more conspicuously because of the naked branches around. The life within is too strong to fear the shortened day, the cold blast of the falling snow. So with the man of God whose life is maintained by communion; adversity only brings out the strength and reality of the life within.

The leaf of the tree is no mere adornment. If the root suggests receptive power, the leaves no less remind us of the grace of giving out and of purifying. The thin, stimulating sap that comes from the root could not of itself build up the tree. Through the leaves it possesses itself of carbon from the atmosphere. The tiniest rootlets are as much nourished by the leaves as the latter are fed by the roots. Keep a tree despoiled of its leaves and it will surely die. "Whose leaf does not wither."

- **Uniform prosperity:** "Whatever he does prospers". Could any promise go beyond this? It is the privilege of the child of God to see the hand of God in all his circumstances, and to serve God in all his avocations and duties. And he who in all things recognises himself as the servant of God may count on a sufficiency from God for all manner of need.

But this prosperity will not always be apparent, except to the eye of faith. Doubtless the legions of hell rejoiced when they saw the Lord of Glory nailed to the accursed tree, yet we know that never was our blessed Lord more prosperous than when he offered himself as our atoning sacrifice. The path of real prosperity will often lie through deepest suffering; but followers of Christ may well be content with the path he trod.'

5

The Way of Holiness

Be Holy Because I am Holy

The Apostle Peter wrote, 'Just as he who called you is holy, so be holy in all you do; for it is written: "Be holy, because I am holy."'[15] Hudson Taylor grew up in the Wesleyan tradition. Both sides of his family were Methodists, and as a child he loved to hear stories of the day when his great-grandfather James Taylor had entertained the family's most distinguished visitor. John Wesley himself, then aged eighty-two, visited Barnsley and stayed at his great-grandfather's cottage in June 1786.

A few months after his conversion in 1849 Hudson went through a bad patch when he found it an effort to pray and the Bible seemed dull to read. But one of the things which brought him through this difficult time was an article in the *Wesleyan Magazine* on 'The Beauty of Holiness', which made sheer goodness seem irresistibly attractive. In his prayers he told God, 'My heart longs for this perfect holiness.' And a letter he wrote to his sister at this time reflected John Wesley's language: 'I am seeking entire sanctification.'

Is Perfection Possible?

In a meditation on the words of Christ, 'Be perfect, therefore, as your Heavenly Father is perfect',[16] Hudson Taylor wrote:

'We are to be the salt of the earth and the light of the world, not to break one of the least of the commandments, not to give way to anger, nor to tolerate the thought of impurity, to give no rash promises, or in conversation to say more than yes or no. The spirit of retaliation is not to be indulged in; a yieldingness of spirit is to characterise the child of the kingdom, and those who hate and despitefully use us are to be pitied and prayed for. In the little frictions of daily life, as well as in the more serious trials and persecutions to which the Christian is exposed, he is manifestly to be an imitator of his Heavenly Father.

'Now God's perfection is an absolute perfection, while ours, at best, is only relative. A needle may be a perfect needle, in every way adapted to its work … [but] under the magnifying power [of a microscope] it becomes a rough honeycombed poker. So we are not called to be perfect angels, or in any respect divine, but we are called to be perfect Christians, performing the privileged duties that as such devolve upon us.

'Now our Father makes the least little thing that he creates *according to his perfection*. The tiniest fly, the smallest animalcule, the dust of the butterfly's wing, however highly, you magnify them, are seen as absolutely perfect.'

This reference to an 'animalcule' or 'microscopic animal', which is typical of many in Hudson Taylor's writings, reminds us of his intense interest in natural history, photography, microscopy and dissection which his father encouraged in his youth and which Hudson retained all his life.

'Should not the little things of daily life be as relatively perfect in the case of the Christian as lesser creations of God are perfect as his work? Ought we not to glorify God in the formation of each letter that we write, and to write a more legible hand as Christians than unconverted people can be expected to do? Ought we not to be more thorough in our service, not simply doing well that which will be seen and noticed, but, just as our Father makes many a flower to bloom unseen in the lonely desert, so to do all that we can do as under his eye, though no other eye may take note of it?'

If Only I Could Abide in Christ

In the summer months of 1869 when Hudson Taylor was thirty-seven, his morale was low and irritability was his 'daily hourly failure'. Sometimes he even wondered whether someone so dogged by failure could be a Christian at all. Long periods of separation from his wife Maria, and a bout of severe illness, didn't help.

With all this went a sense of need. He saw it as a need both for himself and for the mission of more holiness, life and power. He believed the personal need was greater: 'I felt the ingratitude, the danger, the sin of not living nearer to God.'

He prayed, he agonised, he fasted, he tried to do better, and he made resolutions. He read the Bible more carefully. He ordered his life to give more time for rest and meditation. But all this had little effect.

Looking back on the period a few months later he wrote: 'every day, almost every hour, the consciousness of sin oppressed me. I knew that if only I could abide in Christ all would be well, but I *could not*. I began the day with prayer, determined not to take my mind off him for a moment; but pressure of duties, sometimes very trying, constant interruptions apt to be so wearing, often caused me to forget him . . . Each day brought its register of sin and failure, of lack of power. To will was indeed present with me, but how to perform I found not.'

He began to ask himself whether the rest of his Christian life would be one of constant conflict and, instead of victory, regular defeat. How could he preach with sincerity that to all who received Jesus, 'He gave the right to become children of God'[17] [that is God-like] when this wasn't his experience?

Instead of growing stronger, he seemed to be growing weaker and giving in more to sin. He hated himself; he hated his sin. Throughout the period, as he recalled at the time, 'I felt assured that there was in Christ all I needed, but the practical question was how to get it *out*.' With the biblical picture of Christ as the vine[18] on his mind, he wrote, 'He was rich, truly, but I was poor; he strong, but I weak. I knew full well that there was in the root, the stem, abundant fatness; but how to get it into my puny little branch was the question.'

Transforming Insights

Gradually Hudson Taylor began to gain insights which were to bring him through this period. First, he saw that *faith* was the precondition for gaining what he wanted – it was 'the hand to lay hold on his fullness and make it my own'. But he didn't have this faith. He struggled for it, but it wouldn't come. He tried to exercise it, but in vain

'Seeing more and more the wondrous supply of grace laid up in Jesus, the fullness of our precious Saviour – my help-lessness and guilt seemed to increase. Sins I committed appeared but as trifles compared with the sin of unbelief which was their cause, which could not or would not take at his Word, but rather made him a liar! Unbelief was, I felt the damning sin of the world – yet I indulged in it. I prayed for the faith, but it came not. What was I to do?'

The second insight came in the shape of a letter from fellow-missionary John McCarthy. Taylor had shared with McCarthy something of the turmoils through which he was passing.

'I do wish I could have a talk with you now, about the way of holiness,' McCarthy wrote:

'Do you know, dear brother, I now think that this striving, effort, longing, hoping for better days to come, is not the true way to happiness, holiness or usefulness; better, no doubt far better, than being satisfied with our poor attain-ments, but not the best way after all. I have been struck with a passage from a book of yours left here, entitled *Christ is All*. It says: "The Lord Jesus received is holiness begun; the Lord Jesus cherished is holiness advancing; the Lord Jesus counted upon as never absent would be holi-ness complete . . ." A channel is now formed by which Christ's fullness plenteously flows down. The barren branch becomes a portion of the fruitful stem . . . One life reigns throughout the whole.'

'Believer, you mourn your shortcomings; you find the hated monster, sin, still striving for the mastery, help is laid up for you in Christ. Seek clearer interest in him ... He is most holy who has most of Christ within, and joys most fully in the finished work. It is defective faith which clogs the feet, and causes many a fall.

'The last sentence I think I now fully endorse ... How then to have our faith increased? Only by thinking of all that Jesus is, and all he is for us. Not a striving to have faith, or to increase our faith, but a looking off to the Faithful One seems all we need; a resting in the Loved One entirely, for time and for eternity.'

When Hudson Taylor finished reading McCarthy's letter he wrote, 'As I read it I saw it all! "If we are faithless, he will remain faithful."[19] I looked to Jesus and saw (and when I saw, oh, how joy flowed!) that he had said, "I will never leave you." Ah, *there* is rest! I thought, *I have striven in vain to rest in him. I'll strive no more. For has he not promised to abide with me – never to leave me, never to fail me?'*

In the succeeding few days God gave him new insights and clarified his thinking. Faith, he saw, was 'the *substance* of things hoped for, and not mere shadow. It is not *less* than sight, but *more*. Sight only shows the outward forms of things; faith gives the substance. You can *rest* on substance, *feed* on substance. Christ dwelling in the heart by faith . . . is *power* indeed, is life indeed. And Christ and sin will not dwell together; nor can we have his presence with love of the world, or carefulness about "many things".'

Keswick and Holiness

These insights about the relationship between abiding in Christ and holiness were influential in the establishment of the Keswick Convention in 1875. Some of Hudson Taylor's friends expressed reservations to him about overstressing the passive, receptive side of holiness; they underlined the need for active resistance to evil and of effort to obey God. In his books a few years later, Bishop Ryle was also to correct what he considered to be the imbalance of Keswick teaching. And in his book, *Keep in Step with the Spirit*,[20] Dr Jim Packer expressed serious reservations about the Keswick version of holiness. He makes the same point that Hudson Taylor was warned about at the time – that there was, and is, a danger of over emphasising the passive side of holiness.

Defining passivity as 'conscious inaction' Dr Packer writes:

'Souls that cultivate passivity do not thrive but waste away. The Christian's motto should not be "Let go and let God" but "Trust God and get going!" So if, for instance, you are fighting a bad habit, work out before God a strategy for ensuring that you will not fall victim to it again, ask him to bless your plan, and go out in his strength, ready to say *no* next time the temptation comes. Or if you are seeking to form a good habit, work out a strategy in the same way, ask God's help, and then try your hardest. But passivity is never the way, and the overtones of passivity in Keswick teaching ("Don't struggle with it yourself, just hand it over to the Lord") are unbiblical in themselves and hostile to Christian maturity.'

The crux of Hudson Taylor's insight in 1869 was that faith in Christ, looking to him, was as essential an ingredient in the pursuit of holiness as it is in our salvation. But it is not, of course, a sufficient ingredient and it is likely (judging from his other writings), that Hudson Taylor would have agreed that we should never encourage a Christian to believe either that there is any quick or easy shortcut along the way of holiness (a danger Dr Packer sees in some charismatic circles as well as in Keswick teaching), or that the experience of sanctification will not involve a struggle.

Taylor's colleague John McCarthy pointed out that striving to achieve holiness in our own strength, though inadequate, is at least better than being satisfied with our poor attainments. There is no evidence that Hudson Taylor and his colleagues in China were deficient in effort or active service. We have already seen Taylor's warning to potential candidates for his mission that if they didn't intend to 'walk blamelessly'[21] they'd do better to stay at home.

'We are nowhere taught,' Hudson Taylor wrote at another time, 'that abiding in Christ implies sinlessness. On the other hand, if abiding is not sinlessness, neither is it compatible with any known sin. "I write this to you that you will not sin."'[22]

The Consequences of Sin

Sin is an unfashionable subject today, although we needn't delve deep into the pages of either our newspaper or our Bible before we come across it and its consequences. Scripture uses a variety of words to speak of sin, with meanings ranging from 'the missing of a mark or goal' or 'the breach of a relationship' to 'ungodliness', 'perversion' or 'rebellion'; yet the common theme of every biblical expression of the nature of sin is the idea that sin separates us from the holy God.

Hudson Taylor believed that the enormity of sin, and the awful consequences which result from it, were not sufficiently understood or taught in his day. This is a message which is also needed today. 'The world is a hard master' he wrote, 'and sin, even if forgiven, is never undone; its consequences remain. The sin of David was forgiven, but the prophet who announced the pardon was commissioned to tell him that the sword would never depart from his house. Every sin committed is a seed sown, and abides in its consequences; and, however secret it may have been, it shall, as the Saviour teaches, be brought to light. This truth needs emphasis in the present day, even among the children of God . . .'

'Because God graciously promises that forgiven sin shall be no more remembered against the believer, many forget that God's Word equally assures us that "God will bring every deed into judgement, including every hidden thing, whether it is good or evil",[23] a passage the force of which has not passed away under the new dispensation; for the Lord himself endorses it, saying: "There is nothing concealed that will not be disclosed, or hidden that will not be made known."[24] And Paul says: "We must all appear before the judgement seat of Christ."[25]

'And not only so; for even in this life there is a reaping, in measure, of that which is sown, which may come from the hands of men, who are often God's sword to chasten his children.'

Christ Comes in the Written Word

When Hudson Taylor was a child, his father would take him and his sisters into his bedroom once a day, kneel at the four-poster bed and pray with each of them. Then the children would be sent to their own rooms to read their Bibles for a while. 'Learn to love your Bible,' their father said. 'God cannot lie. He cannot mislead you. He cannot fail.'

Hudson Taylor accepted both the assessment and the advice, and spent a lifetime soaking himself in the Scriptures.

He stressed a close connection between the incarnate and the written Word. Among the verses which, he argued, established this link were John 15:7: 'If you remain in me and my words remain in you, ask whatever you wish, and it will be given you'.

'Our Saviour does not say, "Remain in me, and I in you," but "if you remain in me and my *words* remain in you." The substitution of "my words" for the "I" in verse 4 brings out the close connection between the incarnate and the written Word. To us Christ comes in the written Word, brought home to the soul by the Holy Spirit. As we feed upon the written Word, we feed on the living Christ.

'We must take time to be holy. It is not so much the quantity of Scripture we read, as the subjects for meditation which we find in it, that measure the nourishment we gain. On the other hand our reading must not be too limited; for as the whole Paschal Lamb was to be eaten, so the whole Word of God is profitable and necessary "so that the man of God may be thoroughly equipped for every good work."[26] We would earnestly recommend the consecutive reading of the whole Word of God to all who do not read it; and, to all who are able to do so, that the whole Bible be read over in the course of the year. Where this cannot be done prayerfully and thoughtfully, rather let a shorter portion be taken for daily reading, still going through the whole of the Word consecutively.

'The verse before us[27] shows the important connection existing between a full knowledge of the Word of God and successful prayer. Those prayers only will be answered which are in harmony with the revealed will of God. Many of us have heard earnest, but ignorant, prayers for things clearly contrary to the revealed purposes of God. Again a full knowledge of the Word will often bring to our recollection appropriate promises, and thus enable us to pray with faith and confidence.

'Abiding in Christ and feeding upon his Word will lead to a Christ-like walk, which will assure our hearts before God.'

The Source of Power

One of Hudson Taylor's favourite verses, which he often referred to when preaching, was Psalm 62:11: 'God hath spoken once; twice have I heard this; that power belongeth unto God.'[28]

'God himself is the great source of power' he said. 'It is his possession. Power belongeth unto God, and he manifests it according to his sovereign will. Yet, not in an erratic or arbitrary manner, but according to his declared purpose and promises. True, our opponents and hindrances are many and mighty, but our God, the living God, is almighty.'

'God tells us by his prophet Daniel, that the people who know their God shall be strong and do exploits.[29] It is ordinarily true that knowledge is power; it is supremely true in the case of the knowledge of God. Those who know their God do not *attempt* to do exploits, but *do* them. We shall search the Scriptures in vain for any command to *attempt* to do anything. God's commands are always "Do this". If the command be from God, our only course is to obey.

'Further, God's power is *available* power. We are supernatural people, born again by a supernatural birth, kept by a supernatural power, sustained on supernatural food, taught by a supernatural teacher from a supernatural book. We are led by a supernatural captain in right paths to assured victories. The risen Saviour, before he ascended on high, said: "All power is given unto Me. Go ye therefore . . ."[30]

'Again, he said to his disciples: "You will receive power when the Holy Spirit comes on you."[31] Not many days after this, in answer to united and continued prayer, the Holy Spirit did come upon them, and they were all filled. Praise God, he remains with us still. This power given is not a gift from the Holy Spirit. He himself is the power. Today he is truly available, and as mighty in power as he was on the day of Pentecost. But since the days before Pentecost has the whole Church ever put aside every other work and waited on God for ten days that the power might be manifested? We have given too much attention to method, and to machinery, and to resources, and too little to the source of power.'

Walking in the Spirit

Hudson Taylor trusted the power of the Holy Spirit. When he recalled his own conversion, he recorded that 'light was flashed into my soul by the Holy Spirit' and for the next fifty-six years, through success and failure, victory and defeat, he sought to walk in the Spirit. During the last thirty years of his life, the Holy Spirit features particularly prominently in his writing and recorded addresses.

The summer of 1873 was extremely difficult for Hudson Taylor. He badly wanted an administrator in China who would leave him free for pioneering missionary work, evangelism and church planting; two CIM missionaries, William and Mary Rudland, were proving difficult to handle; some Chinese assistants were demanding higher wages; and there was an outbreak of anti-foreign and anti-Christian feeling in the area. In a note to Jennie, his second wife, Hudson wrote, 'Oh for a baptism of the Holy Spirit . . . the only remedy for our troubles.'

At other times, Hudson Taylor spoke of the mission's need for the 'manifested presence' of the Holy Spirit; the 'filling' of the Spirit; of individuals being 'channels' of the Spirit; 'receiving' the Spirit; and an 'outpouring', 'giving' and 'coming to power' of the Spirit. The variety of terms used rightly reflects the uncontrollability of the Spirit who hovered over the waters at creation and who, like the wind, blows wherever he pleases.

Divine Power, not Machinery

In March 1892 Taylor issued an important circular to every member of the CIM. After reporting recent conversions in Shanghai, he wrote: 'The supreme need of all missions in the present day is the manifested presence of the Holy Spirit . . .'

'Few of us, perhaps, are satisfied with the results of our work, and some may think that if we had more, or more costly machinery we should do better. But oh, I feel that it is *divine power* we want and not machinery! If the tens and thousands we now reach daily are not being won for Christ, where would be the gain in machinery that would enable us to reach double the number? Should we not do well, rather, to suspend our present operations and give ourselves to humiliation and prayer for nothing less than to be filled with the Spirit, and made channels through which he shall work with resistless power?

'Souls are perishing now for lack of power . . . God is blessing now some who are seeking this blessing from him in faith. All things are ready, if we are ready. Let us ask him to search us and remove all that hinders his working in us in large measure . . . And having sought the removal of all hindrances and yielded ourselves up in fresh consecration, let us accept by faith the filling and definitely receive the Holy Spirit, to occupy and govern the cleansed temple.'

On 16 April 1892, the proceedings of the CIM's China Council were suspended. The minutes of the meeting record that, 'Instead of meeting for conference, the China Council united with members of the mission in Shanghai seeking for themselves, the whole mission in China and the Home Councils, the filling of the Holy Spirit.'

The Council's prayers were answered. 'God is working in our midst,' Jennie wrote that same month, 'emptying and humbling one and another, and filling with the Holy Spirit. We are having frequent meetings full of liberty and power.'

Whoever Drinks

Hudson Taylor said that as the Son came to reveal the Father, so the Spirit came to reveal the Son. 'Christ was a true Comforter, and the Holy Spirit is the other Comforter, sent by the Father in Christ's name, that he might abide with the Church forever. Christ is the indwelling Saviour; the Holy Spirit the indwelling Comforter. On whomsoever Christ makes his face to shine, the Holy Spirit will surely lift up his countenance.'

'We shall never forget,' he wrote at another time, 'the blessing we received through the words, "whoever drinks the water I give him will never thirst."[32] So we realised that Christ literally meant what he said – that "will" meant will, and "never" meant never, and "thirst" meant thirst – our heart overflowed with joy as we accepted the gift. Oh, the thirst with which we sat down, but oh, the joy with which we sprang from that seat, praising the Lord that the thirsting days were all past, and past for ever! For, as our Lord continues: "The water I give him will become in him a spring of water welling up to eternal life."[33]

'Perhaps however we should draw attention to the words of Christ: "whoever drinks" not "drank" – once for all but "drinks", that is habitually. After promising that out of him "streams of living water will flow" it is ended: "by this he meant the Spirit, whom those who believed in him"[34] – that is, keep believing – "were later to receive."'

John Stott made the same point, commenting on the same verses, one hundred years later in his booklet *The Baptism and Fullness of the Holy Spirit*.[35]

To Whom Does God Give his Spirit?

Hudson Taylor was invited to preach the opening sermon at the General Missionary Conference in the spring of 1890. When he addressed this large audience in Shanghai, drawn from all the Protestant societies working in China, he spoke for an hour and departed from his prepared address with a passage on the power of the Holy Spirit.

He referred to the Lord's final command to his disciples to preach the gospel 'to every creature' and went on to quote from the Apostle Peter's address to the Sanhedrin when he spoke of the Holy Spirit 'whom God has given to those who obey him.'[36]

'If as an organised conference, we were to set ourselves to obey the command of the Lord to the full, we should have such an outpouring of the Holy Spirit, such a Pentecost as the world has never seen since the Holy Spirit was outpoured in Jerusalem. God gives his Spirit not to those who long for him, not to those who pray for him, not to those who desire to be filled always – but he does give his Holy Spirit to them that obey him.

'If as an act of obedience we were to determine that every district, every town, every village, every hamlet in this land should hear the gospel, and that speedily, and were to set about doing it, I believe that the Spirit would come down in such mighty power that we would find supplies springing up we know not how. We should find the fire spreading from missionary to flock, and our native fellow-workers and the whole Church of God would be blessed. God gives his Holy Spirit to them that obey him.'

6.

The Mystery of Prayer

Praying and Working

Hudson Taylor believed in the power of prayer. His life as a Christian had begun in answer to his mother's specific prayers. And his response to God's call to serve him in China was itself an answer to a prayer offered by his parents before his birth. It is not surprising therefore that his own life was characterised by prayer.

One missionary with whom he travelled in the summer of 1877 never forgot his habit of praying for the mission three times a day, mentioning each of his colleagues by name.

His son Howard noticed that his father, 'prayed about things as if everything depended on the praying . . . but worked also, as if everything depended on the working.' A classic example of this occurred in 1870 during one of Taylor's spells in England. On 31 December the CIM observed a day of prayer at the mission's headquarters in Pyrland Road at a time when many small children were dying of 'spasmodic croup'. During the evening session, a nurse appeared at the door with a child she thought had died. They called Taylor, who rushed to the back of the room. As he ran, a woman suggested that he should pray. 'Yes, pray,' he shouted back, 'while I work!'

Taylor found that the small girl was blue and limp. His first efforts to revive her failed. Then he tried the kiss of life. After several minutes, the child's colour changed and she began to breathe. In the night she had occasional convulsions but survived without harm, and grew up to be a CIM missionary.

Our Prayers are Answered Now!

Late in 1886, the idea of praying the ambitious prayer that one hundred new missionaries would join the mission during 1887, was born. A veteran Shanghai missionary said to Hudson Taylor, 'I am delighted to hear that you are praying for large reinforcements. You will not get a hundred of course, within the year; but you will get many more than if you did not ask for them.'

'Thank you for your interest,' Taylor replied. 'We have the joy of knowing our prayers answered now. And I feel sure that if spared, you will share the joy of welcoming the last of the 'hundred to China!'

Back in England during 1887, Taylor spent an incredibly busy year addressing hundreds of meetings; dealing with an enormous correspondence; interviewing hundreds of candidates who were anxious to go to China; facing opposition from the CIM's London Council; and advising his deputy in China on detailed administrative problems.

By early November, Taylor was able to announce that one hundred and two candidates had been accepted for service with the CIM, and that enough money had been given to pay for their passages to China. The figure of one hundred and two included two associate missionaries, so that God not only answered the many prayers, but answered them with total precision!

Among those who welcomed the last of the hundred was the elderly missionary who had felt so sure that the mission's prayers would not be completely answered.

Sympathies as Broad as the World

Hudson Taylor didn't confine himself to praying for China. Dr Harry Guinness, Director of the Regions Beyond Missionary Union, noticed that Taylor 'was always praying for South America . . . His sympathies were as broad as the world, and it was South America every time he prayed.' Another friend commented: 'It was just as much joy to him when men went to Africa or to Japan, or to India . . . Persia . . . as it was when they went to China . . . It was the world that he wanted for Christ.'

Does God Always Answer Prayer?

Hudson Taylor often preached from 2 Corinthians 12:1-10 where the Apostle Paul refers intriguingly to the occasion when he had been 'caught up in the third heaven' and 'heard inexpressible things, things that a man is not permitted to tell.' The Apostle believed that to keep him from becoming conceited following these unusual experiences he had been given a 'thorn in the flesh' – an illness or handicap perhaps, the nature of which we can only guess at – but which Paul saw as a messenger of Satan. 'Three times' wrote Paul, 'I pleaded with the Lord to take it away from me. But he said to me, "My grace is sufficient for you, for my power is made perfect in weakness."'[37] The Apostle drew the right conclusion: 'For when I am weak, then I am strong.'

Hudson Taylor said that the Apostle, 'knew himself to be in just the very position to be made a blessing to others. His unanswered: and yet his request as not granted as he asked it.

'Do we not get, both in the case of the Lord Jesus and of the Apostle Paul, much light on the question so often asked: "Does God *always* answer prayer?" There are of course many prayers that he does not answer – prayers that are asked amiss, that are contrary to God's revealed will, or that are unmixed with faith. But there are many other prayers that are proper petitions, offered in a proper spirit, in which nevertheless the answer does not come just in the way the offerer may have expected. When a great need is brought to God in prayer, he may answer the prayer by supplying the need or removing it: just as we may balance a pair of scales, adding to the light scale or reducing the weight of the heavier. Paul was distressed by a burden which he had not strength to bear, and asked that the burden might be removed. God answered the prayer, not by taking it away, but by showing him the power and the grace to bear it joyfully. Thus that which had been the cause of sorrow and regret now became the occasion of rejoicing and triumph.

'And was not this really a *better* answer to Paul's prayer than the mere removing of the thorn? The latter course would have left him open to the same trouble when the next distress came; but God's method at once and for ever delivered him in *all* the oppression of the present and of all future similar trials. Hence he triumphantly exclaims: "Therefore I will boast all the more gladly about my weaknesses, so that Christ's power may rest on me."[38] Ah! I would not wish to share in the Apostle's thorn in the flesh, if thereby he might be brought in reality into the experience of his deliverance from the oppression of all weakness, all injury, all necessity, all persecution, all distress; and might henceforth know that the very hour and time of weakness was the hour and time of truest strength? Let none fear then to step out in glad obedience to the Master's commands.'

A Divinely Appointed Means of Grace

When Hudson Taylor visited Shanxi, a northern province of China, he met Chinese Christians who were in the habit, alone and together, of regularly spending time in fasting and prayer. He discovered that 'they recognised that this fasting, which so many dislike, which requires faith in God, since it makes one feel weak and poorly, is really a divinely appointed means of grace. Perhaps the greatest hindrance to our work' he continued, 'is our imagined strength; and in fasting we learn what poor weak creatures we are – dependent on a meal of meat for the little strength which we are so apt to lean upon. However the blessing comes, this I know: we do find that when we have had a serious difficulty in the CIM, and set apart a day of fasting (we have had very many) God always interposes. He goes before us, and makes crooked places straight: he goes before us and makes rough places plain.'

7

Respecting the Culture

Why Wear Chinese Clothes?

Within a year of arriving in China, Hudson Taylor had begun seriously to consider the possibility of wearing Chinese dress. His understanding of the case for taking this step was rooted in his deep respect for Chinese culture and his sensitive perception of the role of the missionary, in which he was far ahead of his time. He pointed out that Chinese customs had developed over thousands of years; and that those who knew the Chinese best came to appreciate that the need for traditional Chinese customs originated in the climate, history and geography of the country.

He argued that there was 'perhaps no country in the world where religious toleration is carried out to so great an extent as in China.' The only reason, he said, that the Chinese at every level of society objected to Christianity was that to them it was a foreign religion which tended to mould converts into the ways of foreign nations.

Respect for Chinese Culture

Taylor's regard for the Chinese people, their culture and morality was well illustrated in an article he wrote for *China's Millions*[39] in 1875. He referred to the evil influence of the large western and nominally Christian community, which had grown up around the Chinese ports, among whom were many whose lives, he said, were 'less moral than those of the heathen around them'.

To Hudson Taylor, the main obstacles to a rapid acceptance of Christianity by large numbers of Chinese were to do with the missionaries – and sometimes their converts – wearing European clothes and the practice of building western-style churches. He could see no justification either in Scripture or reason for giving Chinese Christianity a western flavour: 'It is not their denationalisation but their Christianisation that we seek'.

What he wanted to see were 'Christian Chinese – true Christians, but withal Chinese in every sense of the word. We wish to see churches and Christian Chinese presided over by pastors and officers of their own countrymen, worshipping their true God in the land of their fathers, in the custom of their fathers, in their own tongue wherein they were born, and in edifices of a thoroughly Chinese style of architecture . . . Let us in everything unsinful become Chinese, that by all means we may save some. Let us adopt their costume, acquire their language, study to imitate their habits, appropriate to their diet as far as health and constitution will allow. Let us live in their houses, making no unnecessary alterations to external appearance, and only so far modifying internal arrangements as attention to health and efficiency for work absolutely require.

'In Chinese dress, the foreigner, though recognised as such, escapes the mobbing and crowding to which, in many places, his own costume would subject him; and in preaching, while his dress attracts less notice his words attract more. He can purchase articles of dress and also get them washed and repaired without difficulty and at a trifling expense in any part of the country.'

These were the ideas, and this was the vision, that inspired Hudson and Maria, his first wife, in their work. They passionately believed that the Chinese would only be won for Christ if those who brought them the gospel from the West understood and respected their ancient culture.

The Sort of Commitment the CIM Expected

Home in England in 1868, William Berger was weighed down with the task of interviewing and selecting new candidates for the mission. Hudson Taylor wrote to him:

'We, as a mission, differ from all the other missions. As soon as some persons arrive here they find a sufficient answer to every question in, "the American missionaries do this, or the Church missionaries do that; why can't we …?"

'The missionaries of almost all the societies have better houses, finer furniture, more European fare than we have or are likely to have. But there is not one of them settled in the interior among the people. Unless persons are prepared to stand alone – separate from these societies and those who imitate them – they should never join our mission at all … Let them know, too, beforehand, that if they are hearty, loyal members of this mission, they may expect the sneers and even opposition of good, godly men.'

He went on to give clear and unambiguous advice to William Berger:

'I only desire the help of such persons as are fully prepared to work in the interior, in the native costume, and living, as far as possible, in the native style. I do not contemplate assisting, in future, any who may cease to labour in this way. China is open to all; but my time and strength are too short, and the work too great to allow of my attempting to work with any who do not agree with me in the main on my plans of action ...

'China is not to be won for Christ by quiet, ease-loving men and women ... The stamp of men and women we need is such as will put Jesus, China, souls, first and foremost in everything and at every time – even life itself must be secondary ... Of such men, and such women, do not fear to send us too many. They are more precious than rubies.'

A Chinese Church

Hudson Taylor's strategy was to make the CIM's work more and more, as he put it, native and interior with as few foreign workers as possible. His eventual aim was to have one superintendent and two assistant foreign missionaries in a province, with Chinese helpers in each important city, and Bible distributors in the less important places. He also planned to open a college to train Chinese workers.

He was delighted to find that Chinese Christians were growing more and more efficient in the work of evangelism and church building, and had no doubt that the future of the Church in China lay with them. 'I look on all us foreign missionaries as a platform work round a rising building,' he wrote: 'The sooner it can be dispensed with the better; or rather, the sooner it can be transferred to other places, to serve the same temporary purpose, the better for the work efficiently forward to dispense with it, and the better for the places yet to be evangelised.' This approach remains key to missionary strategy today.

To Help Not to Lord

Writing in the CIM's *Book of Arrangements* about leadership, Taylor said, 'The principle of godly rule is a most important one, for it equally affects us all. It is this – the seeking to help, not to lord; to keep from wrong paths and lead into right paths, for the glory of God and the good of those guided, not for the gratification of the ruler. Such rule always leads the ruler to the Cross, and saves the ruled at the cost of the ruler . . . When the heart is right it loves godly rule, and finds freedom in obedience.'

Giving advice to his deputy John Stevenson, Hudson Taylor recommended that 'so long as you continue to seek his guidance in every matter and in the midst of the presence of work take time to be holy and take time to pray for the workers, the Lord will continue to use and own and bless you.'

Taylor was a flexible leader and knew when to waive his own rules. In the summer of 1894, he and Jennie (his second wife) travelled to Xian, the capital of Shanxi, where they spent some time with Scandinavian associates of the CIM. The Scandinavians had been criticised because their party included unmarried women working in some places without male missionaries to help them; a Shanghai newspaper said that this would appear perplexing and perhaps scandalous to the Chinese with their different customs. On his visit, Taylor agreed guidelines governing the behaviour of the women missionaries, and waived the rule forbidding marriage until after two years service in China.

A Social Gospel?

Hudson Taylor's response to one of the worst famines the world had known, illustrates the balance which he succeeded in striking between preaching the gospel and responding to wider physical and social needs as they arose. The famine, caused by prolonged drought and a failure of wheat and other crops, began in Shanxi and spread to other northern provinces of China during the 1870s.

Early in 1877, Taylor wrote an editorial for *China's Millions* on 'Concern for the Poor and Helpless' based on Psalm 41:1-3, 'Blessed is he that considereth the poor: the Lord will deliver him in the time of trouble. The Lord will preserve him, and keep him alive; and he shall be blessed upon the earth.'[40]

'Who, then, will be blessed in this way? Not the one who cheaply relieves his own eyes of a painful spectacle by trifling alms, or relieves himself of the importunity of a collector for some benevolent cause. Not the one who quiets his own conscience by gifts which really cost no self-denial, and then dismisses the case of the poor and needy from his thoughts, complacently claiming the blessings promised to the charitable. As for those who seek fame and name by their gifts, we altogether dismiss their case from consideration.

'Those who would be blessed are those who consider the poor, those who turn their thoughts and attention towards the poor and needy, and those who do what they can, at the cost of personal self-denial, to reduce the sum of human unhappiness.'

Hudson Taylor issued a warning against spiritualising the text of Psalm 41 (and other parts of Scripture) so that it lost its obvious meaning. 'This,' he said, 'we Protestants are often in no small danger of doing. How much of the precious time and strength of our Lord was spent on conferring temporal blessings on the poor, the afflicted and the needy? Such administrations, proceeding from right motives, cannot be lost. They are God-like; they are Christ-like.'

Personal Self-Denial

To Hudson Taylor, action 'at the cost of personal self-denial' was the measure of true concern. At his instigation the Wuchang and Ningbo Conferences of Missionaries from a number of societies in China contributed famine relief funds to supplement the funds granted by the Chinese Government.

Taylor sailed for England in November 1877 and launched an appeal for famine relief as soon as he reached home. Britain was slow to react to appeals by the Lord Mayor of London, the Archbishop of Canterbury and the leading missionary societies. Taylor pointed out that England's revenue from the sale of opium 'which is ruining China would exceed in two days all we have yet given to relieve the suffering of the Chinese.' He devoted fourteen pages of one of the issues of *China's Millions* to the famine.

During 1878 Taylor publicised the situation in meetings and in the press, and donations came in for famine relief rather than mission purposes. Even so, he authorised missionaries in famine and relief areas to take in two hundred destitute children, giving priority to orphans. But he wanted to do more: only four months after a long separation from Jennie, he made a painful suggestion.

'You know that I can't leave Britain yet. Would you consider going with a party of new missionaries, and supervising the orphanage scheme until I can come to join you?'

Jennie, now thirty-five with two children aged two and three, prayed about it for two weeks and decided to go. Along with two single women, she travelled under male escort to the capital of Shanxi and worked there for a while assisting orphans and refugees. Although the orphanage was closed later, Jennie and her colleagues had two major achievements to their credit. They took the love of Christ to hundreds suffering the effects of a disastrous famine; and demonstrated that there was no insuperable obstacle in the way of women, married or single, living in inland China.

The First Priority

During a week of meetings for missionaries in the province of Shanxi, Taylor addressed them on the subject of priorities. These messages were recorded in the book *Days of Blessings*, by Montague Beauchamp.

'When God's grace is triumphant in my soul' Taylor said, 'and I can look a Chinaman in the face and say, "God is able to save you, where and as you are" that is when I have power. How else are you going to deal with a man under the craving for opium? The cause of lack of success is very often that we are only half-saved ourselves. If we are fully saved and confess it, we shall see results . . .'

'Let us feel that everything that is human, everything outside the sufficiency of Christ, is only helpful in the measure in which it enables us to bring the soul to him. Our medical missions draw people to us, and we can present to them the Christ of God, medical missions are a blessing; but to substitute medicine for the preaching of the gospel would be a profound mistake. If we put schools or education in the place of spiritual power to change the heart, it will be a profound mistake. If we get the idea that people are going to be converted by some educational process, instead of by a regenerative recreation, it will be a profound mistake. Let all our auxiliaries be auxiliaries – means of bringing Christ and the soul into contact – then we may be truly thankful for them all . . . Let us exalt the glorious gospel in our hearts, and believe that it is the power of God unto salvation. Let everything else sit at its feet . . . We shall never be discouraged if we realise that in Christ is our sufficiency.'

8.

The Sweet Fruit of the Cross

Obsessed with the Cross?

In the weeks leading up to Easter 1995, many British Christians were disturbed to read that the cross had been dropped from a national religious advertising campaign on the grounds that it carried 'too much cultural baggage'. *The Times* reported that advertisers considered the cross too predictable for the campaign and that posters would be produced with the word Surprise! replacing what they described as 'tired old slogans'.[41]

The Churches Advertising Network said that it wanted 'to get away from Easter eggs, bunnies and hot cross buns'. The advertising manager who masterminded the campaign was reported as saying: 'What is this obsession with the cross? We are trying to reach those who are currently not interested in the church or the Christian faith. We are trying to meet them where they are, rather than putting out clichéd images which may be disregarded.'

One diocesan communications officer said that traditional Christian symbols 'carried too much cultural baggage. Endlessly repeating biblical quotations will cut no ice. People have already rejected traditional symbols'. The campaign organisers argued that they had tried in their advertisements to focus on the resurrection, 'to get people outside the church to understand Easter is not just about death but is about resurrection.' They followed the word *Surprise!* in their adverts by the words, 'said Jesus to his friends three days after they buried him . . .'

The resurrection gave Hudson Taylor certain hope for the future. But he could never dispense with the message of the cross which was the source of his salvation, the ground of his joy and the daily pattern of his discipleship.

God's Love in His Heart

He wrote from China to his sister Amelia of his love for God and the place where God's love shines brightest of all

'There is something sublime in contemplating the majesty of God; his wisdom, his power, his omnipresence, too, are themes we love to dwell on – and why? Because we have caught a glimpse – faint it may be, and is – but we have caught a glimpse of the brightness of his glory, have been shown the express image of his person in the face of Jesus Christ, and have learned at Calvary that God is love. This is the reason we now love to dwell on his other attributes, because they are our Father's attributes that is the thought that makes our poor ice-bound hearts glow and burn again – that is the thought that can unseal the fountain of our tears, and melt us in adoring love and gratitude.'

This was a conviction which sustained him throughout his life.

The Best of All Earthly Gifts

In 1857 Hudson fell in love with a much sought after twenty-four-year-old, Maria Dyer, and met violent opposition from sections of the missionary establishment in China. Despite this, the lovers married and spent a three-week honeymoon at a monastery in the hills above Ningbo.

'Oh, to be married to the one you do love' he wrote home, 'and love most tenderly! This is bliss beyond the power of words to express or imagination to conceive. There is no disappointment here. And every day as it shows more of the mind of your beloved, when you have such a treasure as mine, makes you only more proud, more happy, more humbly thankful to the Giver of all good for this the best of all earthly gifts.'

Peopling Heaven with those we Love

When eight-year-old Gracie, Hudson Taylor's daughter, was very sick with meningitis, Hudson wrote to William Berger:

'Beloved brother – I don't know how to write to you, nor how to refrain. I seem to be writing almost from the inner chamber of the King of Kings – surely this is holy ground. I am striving to write a few lines from the side of a couch on which my darling little Gracie lies dying … Dear brother, our heart and flesh fail, but God is the strength of our heart, and our portion for ever. It was no vain or unintelligent act, when knowing the land, its people and climate, I laid my dear wife and the darling children with myself on the altar for this service.'

Four days later, Grace showed signs of pneumonia.

On Friday evening, 23 August, the Taylor family and those closest to them gathered round Grace's bed. Hudson began one hymn after another, though at times his voice failed. Maria sat bent over Grace, now unconscious. At twenty minutes to nine her breathing stopped. 'I never saw anything look so lovely as dear little Gracie did the evening following her death,' Mary Bowyer wrote, 'the sweetest expression of countenance one could behold on earth.'

'Our dear little Gracie!' wrote Hudson. 'How I miss her sweet voice in the morning, one of the first sounds to greet us when we woke – and through the day and at eventide! As I take the walks I used to take with her tripping at my side, the thought comes anew like a throb of agony; is it possible that I shall never more feel the pressure of the little hand, never more hear the sweet prattle of those dear lips, and never more see the sparkle of those bright eyes? And yet she is not lost. I would not have her back again . . . The Gardener came and plucked a rose.'

Less than three years later, two more Taylor children died; followed tragically, by Maria herself at the age of thirty-three. Hudson Taylor sat alone with his thoughts in a house high above Zhenjiang. Separated from his four surviving children he wrote:

'A few months ago, my house was full, now so silent and lonely – Samuel, Noel, my precious wife with Jesus; the elder children far, far away, and even little Charles in Yangzhou. Often, of late years, has duty called me from my loved ones, but I have returned, and so warm has been the welcome. Now I am alone. Can it be that there is no return from this journey, no home-coming to look forward to! Is it real, and not a sorrowful dream, that those dearest to me lie beneath the cold sod? Ah, it is indeed true, but not more so than there is a home-coming awaiting me which no parting shall break into . . . "I go to prepare a place for you." Is not part of the preparation the peopling it with those we love?'

Self-Denial

December 1882, a spell of service in China had kept Hudson Taylor apart from Jennie, his second wife, for fourteen months. He wrote saying that he hoped it wouldn't be long before they were reunited, and asked the agonised question, 'Is anything of value in Christ's service which costs little?'

Jesus said, 'If anyone would come after me, he must deny himself and take up the cross daily and follow me.'[42] Commenting on this verse, Hudson Taylor wrote:

'We might naturally have thought that if there is one thing in the life of the Lord Jesus Christ which belonged to him alone, it was his cross-bearing. To guard against so natural a mistake the Lord Jesus teaches us that if any man will be his disciple he must – not he may – deny himself, and take up his cross daily and follow his Lord.

'Is there not a needs-be for this exhortation? Are not self-indulgence and self-assertion temptations to which we are ever exposed and to which we constantly give way without even a thought of the un-Christ-likeness of such conduct? Self-denial surely means something far greater than some slight and insignificant lessening of self-indulgence!

'As believers, we claim to have been crucified together with Christ; and Paul understood this, not imputatively but practically. He does not say, "I take up my cross daily" in the light modern sense of the expression; he put it rather as dying daily; and therefore, as one "in deaths often", he was never surprised, or stumbled, by any hardship or danger involved in his work.'

What about our Rights?

Writing in *The Times*,[43] the journalist Paul Johnson noted that: 'Traditional societies were duty based because they were religion based. Strictly speaking in a society such as medieval Christendom, no one had rights. Only God had rights. The rest had duties, to God and to each other ... Unfortunately, there is a fatal weakness in any system based on rights.' Many observers agree with Mr Johnson that there is today too much emphasis on rights, and not enough on duties.

Hudson Taylor made the same point in his day. 'What does the Word of God teach us about our rights, our claims, and our dues?' he asked.

'What did our Saviour intend to teach us by the parable of Matthew 18:23-35: "Shouldn't you have had mercy on your fellow-servant just as I had on you?"[44] Can that slave, under those circumstances, assert and claim his right over his fellow?

'Is not this principle of non-assertion, of this aspect of self-denial, a far-reaching one? Did our Lord claim his right before Pilate's bar, and assert himself; or did his self-denial and cross-bearing go the length of waiting for his Father's vindication? And shall we be jealous of our own honour and rights, as men and citizens of western countries, when what our Master wants is witness to and reflection of his own character and earthly life?'

The Call to Suffer

'If you suffer for doing good and you endure it, this is commendable before God.[45] The Christian calling' Hudson Taylor wrote, 'is as unintelligible and as unattractive to unbelief as was the person and work of our glorious head. In the world's judgment he had no form or comeliness, no beauty that they should desire him. It is possible to receive salvation and eternal life through Christ, but with a very imperfect appreciation of the nature, the privileges, and the responsibilities of our calling.

'To what then are we called? To do well, to suffer for it, and to take it patiently.

'"A pretty calling", says Unbelief, and turns away in disgust.

'"Sad, but true", responds many a true but sad heart.

'"I thank you, Father," says Strong Faith, "for so it seemed good in your sight."

'God has not changed since the Holy Spirit recorded the answer to the question given above. Man has not changed; nor has the great enemy of souls changed.

'Now none of the proceedings of God are arbitrary: all the acts and all the requirements of perfect wisdom and of perfect goodness must of necessity be wise and good. We are called when we suffer to take it patiently – and more than patiently, thankfully and joyfully – because seen from a right point of view there is neither ground nor excuse for impatience, but on the contrary abundant cause for overflowing thanks and joy. The early Christians were neither fools nor madmen when they took joyfully the spoiling of their goods, exulting that their names were cast out as evil, and that they themselves were counted worthy to suffer.'

Handling Stress

By the autumn of 1876, Hudson Taylor was complaining that he had four times the amount of work he could do. He had just gone down with dysentery, an illness which recurred throughout his life; on the trip out for his fourth visit to China, his document box containing all the work he had intended to do on the voyage got left behind and after a long delay had now turned up in Zhenjiang; Charles Fisher, secretary to the CIM in China, had returned to England and there was no one else to take his place; the mission's magazine *China's Millions* had to be edited.

At the end of the day – or sometimes at two or three in the morning – Taylor would sit at his harmonium and play his favourite hymns usually getting round to: *Jesus, I am resting, resting, in the joy of what thou art; I am finding out the greatness of thy loving heart*.

On one occasion a fellow-missionary was with him when a pile of letters brought news of dangers and problems facing a number of CIM members. Taylor leaned against his desk to read them and began to whistle, *Jesus, I am resting, resting . . .*

'How can you whistle, when our friends are in such danger?' his colleague asked.

'Suppose I were to sit down here and burden my heart with all these things; that wouldn't help them, and it would unfit me for the work I have to do. I have just to roll the burden on the Lord.'

Unburdened, Strong, Healthy and Happy

Hudson Taylor spent most of 1887 in the United Kingdom, and it was an incredibly busy year for him.

'I'm utterly used up,' he told a colleague at a particularly low moment in the year 'and tempted to wish that my time had come. But he gives power to the faint.'

He celebrated his fifty-fifth birthday on 21 May, and by the 26th the CIM had notched up twenty-one years. During his address at the anniversary meetings, he gave a clue as to how he had learned to cope with all the pressure:

'The Lord's will is that his people should be an unburdened people, fully supplied, strong, healthy and happy … Shall we not determine to be "careful for nothing, but in everything by prayer and supplication with thanksgiving'"'bring those things that would become burdens or anxieties to God in prayer, and to live in his perfect peace?

'. . . I have not known what anxiety is since the Lord taught me that the work is his. My great business in life is to please God. Walking with him in the light, I never feel a burden.'

The Cross Doesn't Get More Comfortable

Sailing towards China with the first batch of North American members of the CIM, Taylor received news of the death of two members of the mission. This was the first of a whole series of heavy blows which led him to write:

'We are passing through wave after wave of trial. Each day has its full quota. God seems daily to be saying, "Can you say, 'even so, Father,' to that?" But he sustains and will sustain the spirit, however much the flesh may fail ... The night and day strain are almost unbearable ... But I know the Lord's ways are all right, and I would not have them otherwise.'

In Shanghai he tried to care for a colleague's daughter who had lost her sanity and tore her clothes and sheets in the next room to him; and members of the London Council and other friends of the mission in England disapproved of his decision to establish a North American branch of the mission. 'Satan is simply raging,' he wrote home to Jennie. 'He sees his kingdom attacked all over the land, and the conflict is awful. But that our Commander is almighty, I should faint. I think I never knew anything like it, though we have passed through some trying times before.'

He had been separated from Jennie for many months now and told her: 'I feel sometimes, drearie, as if the charm and even power of life were taken out of me by these long absences from you . . . Hope deferred makes the heart sick . . . but I cannot shake it off. Longing removes the power of thought . . . The cross does not get more comfortable, does it? But it bears sweet fruit.'

Do Not Worry About Tomorrow

'I will go before you and will level the mountains. [46] This message,' wrote Hudson Taylor, 'is a word of cheer from the Master himself; it has been a feast to my soul and a pillow for my head. It is just as fresh and prized today as it has been in the months that are passed – amongst difficulties that have each seemed to turn to be almost insurmountable.

'Satan would have us try today to bear tomorrow's burden with only today's grace, and would dismay us with anticipation of troubles which loom in the distance, leading us to disobey the directions: "Do not worry about tomorrow",[47] "Do not be anxious about anything";[48] but what a privilege it is to be permitted to rest upon the assurance: "I will go before you; you will not be without a guide", "Whoever follows me will never walk in darkness."[49] "I will level the mountains, and when you come to them you will find insurmountable difficulty already removed, that your enemies, like Jehoshaphat's, have slain themselves, that you have to strip off the spoils", and "O make the valley one, not of conflict, but of praise – a Berachah."

'Again and again it has been so in China, and doubtless many at home can bear the same testimony. A difficulty in the family which they were powerless to cope with, a perplexity in the profession or business, a spiritual difficulty, or one connected with service for the Lord, has threatened to disturb the peace and to fill with dismay, but it has been rolled upon the Lord, and given over to him to manage or arrange; the command has been obeyed: "In everything, by prayer and petition, with thanksgiving, present your requests to God,"[50] and the promised peace of God garrisoning the heart has kept the care and worry outside until the time came to find the trouble bereft of its sting, the mountains levelled. Perhaps there are few who can look back without seeing that such cares as have been borne ought to have been dealt with and dismissed.'

A New Kind of Trial

In November 1898, the 66-year-old Hudson Taylor was travelling in west China with Jennie. The journey took them hundreds of miles up the Yangzi, first by steamer and then by more primitive boats, negotiating mid-winter rapids. About halfway they heard the devastating news of the death of Australian William Fleming, the first CIM martyr, murdered in the south-west province of Guizhou together with his friend and assistant, Pan Shoushan.

'How sad the tidings!' Hudson Taylor wrote to John Stevenson. 'Blessed for the martyrs but sad for us, for China, for their friends. And not only sad, but ominous! It seems to show that God is about to test us with a new kind of trial: surely we need to gird on afresh the whole armour of God. Doubtless it means fuller blessing, but through deeper suffering. May we all lean hard on the Strong for strength . . . and in some way or other the work be deepened and extended, not hindered, by these trials.'

These were prophetic words, heralding the outbreak of the Boxer rebellion, during which many Christians were killed.

A Blessed Sentence to Break Down Upon

In May 1900, Hudson Taylor spoke at a series of meetings in Boston with the American evangelist, Bible teacher and author, Dr A.T. Pierson. At one of these meetings, Taylor seemed to lose his train of thought, and began to repeat two sentences over and over again:

'You may trust the Lord too little, but you can never trust him too much. "If we believe not, yet he abideth faithful: he cannot deny himself." '[51]

Pierson came to the rescue, took over the meeting, and later recorded his reflections on the incident. 'There was something pathetic and poetic in the very fact that this repetition was the first visible sign of his breakdown, for was it not this very sentiment and this very quotation that he had kept repeating to himself, and to all his fellow workers, during all the years of his missionary work? A blessed sentence to break down upon, which had been the buttress of his whole life of consecrated endeavour.'

As he began his convalescence in Switzerland, Taylor said, 'I cannot read; I cannot think; I cannot even pray; but I can trust.'

Enduring Lessons from the Book of Job

Hudson Taylor commented on the book of Job:

'The veil is taken away from the unseen world, and we learn much of the power of our great adversary, but also of his powerlessness apart from the permission of God our Father.

'Satan would very frequently harass the believer in times of sorrow and trial by leading him to think that God is angry with him. But our Heavenly Father delights to trust a trust-worthy child with trial. Take the case of Abraham: God so trusted him that he was not afraid to call upon his servant to offer up his well-beloved son. And in the case of Job, it was not Satan that challenged God about Job, but God who challenged the arch-enemy to find any flaw in his character. In each case grace triumphed, and in each case patience and fidelity were rewarded.'

'The reply of Satan is noteworthy. He had considered God's servant, and evidently knew all about him. The arch-enemy found all his own efforts ineffectual to harass and lead astray God's beloved servant. He found a hedge around him, and about his servants, and about his house, and about all that he had on every side. How blessed to be so protected.

'Is there no analogous spiritual blessing to be enjoyed nowadays? Thank God there is. Every believer may be as safely kept and as fully blessed. The accuser having no fault to find with Job's character or life, insinuates that it is all the result of selfishness. "Does Job fear God for nothing?" Indeed he did not, as Satan well knew! Nor has anyone, before or since. There is no service which pays so well as the service of our Heavenly Master: there is none so royally rewarded. Satan was making a true assertion, the insinuation that it was for the sake of the reward that Job served God, was not true. And to vindicate the character of Job himself, Satan is permitted to test Job.

'And soon Satan shows the malignity of his character by bringing disaster after disaster upon the devoted man.'

Was Job Mistaken?

'God who sent the trial gave also the needful grace, and Job replied to his wife's sneer, "The Lord gave and the Lord has taken away; may the name of the Lord be praised."

'Was not Job mistaken? Should he not have said: "The Lord gave, and Satan has taken away"? No, there was no mistake. He was enabled to discern the hand of God in all these calamities. Satan himself did not presume to ask

God to be allowed himself to afflict Job. He says to God: "Stretch out your hand and strike everything he has, and he will surely curse you to your face." And again: "Stretch out your hand and strike his flesh and bones, and he will surely curse you to your face."

'Satan knew that none but God could touch Job, and Job was quite right in recognising the Lord himself as the doer. Often we shall be helped and blessed if we bear in mind that Satan is servant, and not master, and that he, and wicked men incited by him, are only permitted to do that which God by his determined counsel and foreknowledge has before determined should be done. Come joy or come sorrow, we may always take it from the hand of God.

'Job's kinsfolk failed him, and his familiar friends seem to have forgotten him. Those who dwelt in his house counted him as a stranger, and his servants gave no answer to his calls. Worse than all, his own wife turned from him. No wonder that those who looked on thought that God himself had become his enemy.

'Yet it was not so. With a tender Father's love God was watching all the time; and when the testing had lasted long enough the temporary trial gave place to songs of deliverance.'

Lessons which Prosperity could not Teach

'Nor was the blessing God gave to his servant a small one. During this time of affliction Job learned lessons which all his life of prosperity had been unable to teach him. The mistakes he made in the hastiness of his spirit were corrected; the knowledge of God was deepened and increased. He exclaimed that he had heard of him previously, and knew

God by hearsay only, but that now his eyes saw him, and his acquaintance with God had become personal knowledge. And after all this, Job lived one-hundred-and-forty years, and saw his children and his grandchildren to the fourth generation.

'May we not well say that if Job's prosperity was blessed prosperity, his adversity, likewise, was blessed adversity? "Weeping may remain for the night, but rejoicing comes in the morning";[52] and the night of weeping will bear a fruit more rich and permanent than any day of rejoicing. Light out of darkness is God's order.

'In this day, when material causes are so much dwelt upon that there is a danger of forgetting the unseen agencies, let us not underestimate our unseen foes. It would be comparatively easy to deal with our visible enemies, if the invisible foes were not behind them. We need to put on the whole armour of God, and not to be ignorant of Satan's devices. But let us not lose sight of the precious truth that God alone is Almighty. "If God is for us, who can be against us?"'[53]

God is an Infinite Sovereign

During a difficult and traumatic year, when he had seriously injured his back and had many lonely hours in which to think and pray, Hudson Taylor wrote these words which were unusually challenging, even for him. It was 1874, and he was forty-two at the time, but the meditation, written in his own hand, was only found after his death. As Jim Broomhall has observed, the words 'opened a window on his soul, on the true Hudson Taylor who wanted to be like Christ, cost what it might.'

'If God has called you to be really like Jesus in all your spirit, he will draw you into a life of crucifixion and humility, and put on you such demands of obedience that he will not allow you to follow other Christians; and in many ways he will seem to let other good people do things that he will not let you do. Other Christians and ministers who seem very religious and useful may push themselves, pull wires and work schemes to carry out their schemes, but you cannot do it; and if you attempt it, you will meet such failure and rebuke from the Lord as to make you sorely penitent. Others may brag on themselves, on their work, on their success, on their writings, but the Holy Spirit will not allow you to say any such thing; and if you begin it, he will lead you into some deep mortification that will make you despise yourself and all your good works.

'Others may be allowed to succeed in making money, but it is likely God will keep you poor, because he wants you to have something far better than gold, and that is a helpless dependence on him, that he may have the privilege [the right] of supplying your needs day by day out of an unseen treasury. The Lord will let others be honoured and put forward, and keep you hidden away in obscurity, because he wants some choice fragrant fruit for his coming glory which can be produced in the shade. He will let others do a work for him and get the credit for it, but he will let you work and toil on without [others] knowing how much you are doing; and then to make your work still more precious, he will let others get the credit for the work you have done, and this will make your reward ten times greater when Jesus comes.

'The Holy Spirit will put a strict watch over you, with a jealous love, and will rebuke you for little words or feelings or for wasting your time, over which other Christians never seem distressed. So make up your mind that God is an infinite Sovereign and has a right to do as he pleases with his own and he may not explain to you a thousand things which may puzzle your reason in his dealings with you. He will take you at your word and when you absolutely sell yourself to be his slave, he will wrap you up in a jealous love and let other people say and do many things which he will not let you say or do.

'Settle it for ever that you are to deal directly with the Holy Spirit, and that he is to have the privilege of tying your tongue, or chaining your hand, or closing your eyes, in ways that he does not deal with others. Now when you are so possessed with the living God that you are in the secret heart pleased and delighted over the peculiar, personal, private, jealous guardianship of the Holy Spirit over your life, you will have found the vestibule of Heaven.'

Into the Next Century

Over 100 years after Hudson Taylor's death, the mission he founded (now known as OMF International) not only works in China but throughout East Asia, as well as in a number of other countries where East Asians are found.

OMF's 1200 workers from 30 different nations remain committed to glorifying God through the urgent evangelisation of East Asia's billions. Working closely with local Christians, OMF is committed to evangelism, to reaching those places and people groups where there are no believers and to encouraging and training Christians.

In East Asia's mega-cities, in remote villages and among tribal people, OMF cares for the uncared for; sharing the gospel, planting churches, teaching the Bible, helping the needy and working in partnership with East Asia's Church.

OMF places people of all ages in Asia, from those wanting to serve Christ for a couple of weeks or a gap year, to full-time Christian workers wanting to give their lives to serve God in East Asia. They also place Christians with the right professional skills in countries that do not welcome Bible teachers or evangelists.

Though OMF now works throughout Asia, its values remain the same as in Taylor's day. Its burden to win East Asia for Christ hasn't changed. Its convictions as a faith mission haven't wavered. OMF International continues to pray daily for the provision of all its needs.

As in the days of the China Inland Mission, OMF members take risks and face hardships but hold on to the faithfulness of God, seeking 'first his kingdom and his righteousness' knowing that everything needed will be given.

If you would like to be part of God's work in Asia, or to support OMF International by praying, giving or going, then email omf@omf.org.uk, call 01732 887299 or visit www.omf.org.uk. Contact details for OMF in other countries can be found on page 97 of this book.

Bibliography

Bacon D.W., *From Faith to Faith: The influence of Hudson Taylor on the Faith Missions Movement*, Overseas Missionary Fellowship Books, 1984.

Bonhoeffer D., *The Cost of Discipleship*, Student Christian Movement Press, 2001.

Broomhall A.J., *Hudson Taylor and China's Open Century*, Hodder and Stoughton and the Overseas Missionary Fellowship, Books 1-7, 1981-1990.

Broomhall M., *Hudson Taylor: The Man who believed God*, China Inland Mission, 1929.

Broomhall M. (ed.), *Hudson Taylor's Legacy: Daily Readings*, China Inland Mission, 1931.

Occasional Papers of the China Inland Mission Volumes I-VI. China Inland Mission, 1872.

Packer J.I., *Keep in Step with the Spirit*, Inter-Varsity Press, 1984.

Steer R., *Hudson Taylor: A Man in Christ*, Overseas Missionary Fellowship Books, 1990.

Stott J.R.W., *The Baptism and Fullness of the Holy Spirit*, Inter-Varsity Fellowship, 1964.

Taylor Dr and Mrs Howard, *'By Faith' Henry W Frost and the China Inland Mission*, China Inland Mission, 1938.

Taylor Dr and Mrs Howard, *Hudson Taylor in Early Years: The Growth of a Soul*, China Inland Mission and RTS, 1911.

Taylor Dr and Mrs Howard, *Hudson Taylor and the China Inland Mission: The Growth of a Work of God*, China Inland Mission and RTS, 1918.

Taylor J.H., *China's Spiritual Need and Claims*, Morgan and Scott, 1887.

Taylor J.H., *Retrospect*, Overseas Missionary Fellowship, 1974 .

OMF International works in most East Asian countries, and among East Asian peoples around the world. It was founded by James Hudson Taylor in 1865 as the China Inland Mission. Our purpose is to glorify God through the urgent evangelisation of East Asia's billions.

In line with this, OMF Publishing seeks to motivate and equip Christians to make disciples of all peoples. Publications include:

- Stories and biographies showing God at work in East Asia
- The biblical basis of mission and mission issues
- The growth and development of the church in Asia
- Studies of Asian culture and religion

Books, booklets, articles and free downloads can be found on our website at www.omf.org
Addresses for OMF English-speaking centres can be found on page 97.

Contact Details: OMF

English-Speaking OMF Centres

Australia: PO Box 849, Epping, NSW 1710
Tel: 02 9868 4777 email: au@omf.net
www.au.omf.org

Canada: 5155 Spectrum Way, Building 21, Mississauga,
ONT L4W 5A1
Toll free: 1 888 657 8010 email: omfcanada@omf.ca
www.ca.omf.org

Hong Kong: PO Box 70505, Kowloon Central PO, Hong
Kong
Tel: 852 2398 1823 email: hk@omf.net
www.omf.org.hk

Malaysia: 3A Jalan Nipah, off Jalan Ampang, 55000,
Kuala Lumpur
Tel: 603 4257 4263 email: my@omf.net
www.my.omf.org

New Zealand: PO Box 10159, Dominion Road,
Balmoral, Auckland, 1030
Tel: 09 630 5778 email: omfnz@omf.net
www.nz.omf.org

Philippines: QCCPO Box 1997-1159, 1100 Quezon City,
M.M.
Tel: 632 951 0782 email: ph-hc@omf.net
www.omf.org

Singapore: 2 Cluny Road, Singapore 259570
Tel: 65 6475 4592 email: sno@omf.net
www.sg.omf.org

UK: Station Approach, Borough Green, Sevenoaks,
Kent TN15 8BG
Tel: 01732 887299 email: omf@omf.org.uk
www.omf.org.uk

USA: 10 West Dry Creek Circle, Littleton, CO 80120-
4413
Toll free: 1 800 422 5330 email: omfus@omf.org
www.us.omf.org

OMF International Headquarters: 2 Cluny Road,
Singapore 259570
Tel: 65 6319 4550 email: ihq@omf.net
www.omf.org

Church Bookstalls

For books to build faith in God and to nurture a grasp of his purposes for ourselves, for our nation and for the world, see www.10ofthose.com. We can source all Christian books currently in print at good discounts. Single purchases and bulk purchases available.

For further information please email us at
info@10ofthose.com

Endnotes

[1] Jn. 14:6.
[2] OMF and Authentic Media, reprinted 2005 (available at www.10ofthose.com).
[3] Ps. 84:11 (paraphrased).
[4] SCM Press, 2001.
[5] Mt. 6:33.
[6] Ps. 84:11.
[7] See Lk. 17:5-6.
[8] Mt. 10:29.
[9] Lk. 1:32-33.
[10] Jn. 18:36-37.
[11] 2 Tim. 2:13.
[12] OMF Books, 1984.
[13] See Mt. 6:33.
[14] 2 Tim. 2:13.
[15] 1 Pet. 1:15.
[16] Mt. 5:48.
[17] Jn. 1:12.
[18] Jn. 15: 1-17.
[19] 2 Tim. 2:13.
[20] IVP, 2005.
[21] See Ps. 84:11.
[22] 1 Jn. 2:1.
[23] Ecc. 12:14.

24 Lk. 12:2.
25 2 Cor. 5:10.
26 2 Tim. 3:17.
27 Jn. 15:7.
28 Authorised Version.
29 Dan. 11:32.
30 Mt. 28:18-19, AV.
31 Acts 1:8.
32 Jn. 4:14.
33 Jn. 4:14.
34 Jn. 7:38-39.
35 IVP, 2007 (Reprint).
36 Acts 5:32.
37 2 Cor. 12:8-9.
38 2 Cor. 12:9.
39 *China's Millions* was the journal of the CIM at the time. It is now printed as a magazine called *East Asia's Billions*, available by contacting OMF at www.omf.org.uk.
40 Authorised Version.
41 10 March 1995.
42 Lk. 9:23.
43 24 March 1995.
44 Mt. 18:33.
46 1 Pet. 2:20-21.
47 Is. 45:2.
48 Mt. 6:34.
49 Phil. 4:6.
50 Jn. 8:12.
51 Phil. 4:6.
52 2 Tim. 2:13 AV.
53 Ps. 30:5.
54 Rom. 8:31.